First World War
and Army of Occupation
War Diary
France, Belgium and Germany

31 DIVISION
94 Infantry Brigade
York and Lancaster Regiment
13th (Service) (1st Barnsley) Battalion
1 March 1916 - 28 February 1918

WO95/2365/2

The Naval & Military Press Ltd
www.nmarchive.com
Published in association with The National Archives

Published by

The Naval & Military Press Ltd

Unit 10 Ridgewood Industrial Park,

Uckfield, East Sussex,

TN22 5QE England

Tel: +44 (0) 1825 749494

www.naval-military-press.com

www.nmarchive.com

This diary has been reprinted in facsimile from the original. Any imperfections are inevitably reproduced and the quality may fall short of modern type and cartographic standards.

© **Crown Copyright**
Images reproduced by permission of The National Archives, London, England, 2015.

Contents

Document type	Place/Title	Date From	Date To
Heading	WO95/2365/2		
Heading	31st Division 94th Infy Bde 13th Bn York & Lancaster Regt Mar 1916-Feb 1918 To 93 Bde 31 Div		
War Diary	Kantara	01/03/1916	08/03/1916
War Diary	Port Said	09/03/1916	11/03/1916
War Diary	H.M.T. Megantic	12/03/1916	18/03/1916
War Diary	Railway Train	19/03/1916	19/03/1916
War Diary	Doudelainville	20/03/1916	25/03/1916
War Diary	Fontaine Sur Somme	26/03/1916	26/03/1916
War Diary	Canaples	27/03/1916	27/03/1916
War Diary	Beauval	28/03/1916	28/03/1916
War Diary	Mailly Maillet	29/03/1916	24/06/1916
War Diary	Warnimont Wood Bus	24/06/1916	26/06/1916
Heading	War Diary 13th Battalion The York & Lancaster Regiment July 1916 (30.6.16-31.7.16)		
Heading	War Diary of 13th Bn York & Lancs. Regt. 1st July to 31st July Vol 5		
War Diary	Warnimont Wood	30/06/1916	30/06/1916
War Diary	Bus (Somme)	01/07/1916	01/07/1916
War Diary	Trenches	01/07/1916	04/07/1916
War Diary	Louvencourt	05/07/1916	06/07/1916
War Diary	Gezaincourt	07/07/1916	07/07/1916
War Diary	On The March	08/07/1916	09/07/1916
War Diary	Calonne Sur La Lys	10/07/1916	10/07/1916
War Diary	Le Sart	10/07/1916	14/07/1916
War Diary	Vielle Chapelle	14/07/1916	14/07/1916
War Diary	Trenches	15/07/1916	26/07/1916
War Diary	Vielle Chapelle	27/07/1916	31/07/1916
Heading	War Diary of 13th (S) Bn York & Lancs Regt. Aug 1916 Vol 6		
War Diary	Vielle Chapelle	01/08/1916	04/08/1916
War Diary	Trenches Neuve Chapelle Sector	04/08/1916	04/08/1916
War Diary	Neuve Chapelle	07/08/1916	07/08/1916
War Diary	Sector	08/08/1916	08/08/1916
War Diary	Trenches	09/08/1916	09/08/1916
War Diary	Vielle Chapelle	18/08/1916	26/08/1916
War Diary	Defended Posts	28/08/1916	28/08/1916
War Diary	Neuve Chapelle Sector	31/08/1916	31/08/1916
Heading	War Diary 13th York & Lancaster Regt 31st Division September 1916 Vol 7		
War Diary	Defended Posts Neuve Chapelle Sector	02/09/1916	03/09/1916
War Diary	Trenches	04/09/1916	10/09/1916
War Diary	Lestrem	11/09/1916	15/09/1916
War Diary	Defended Posts Festubert Sector	16/09/1916	23/09/1916
War Diary	Trenches	24/09/1916	24/09/1916
War Diary	Festubert Sector	24/09/1916	26/09/1916
War Diary	Trenches Festubert Sector	24/09/1916	30/09/1916
Heading	War Diary. 13th Bn. York & Lancaster Regt. 31st Division October 1916 Vol 8		
War Diary	Festubert Sector	01/10/1916	01/10/1916

War Diary	Vendin-Lez. Bethune	03/10/1916	03/10/1916
War Diary	Robecq	05/10/1916	05/10/1916
War Diary	Sarton	08/10/1916	17/10/1916
War Diary	Warnimont Wood	18/10/1916	20/10/1916
War Diary	Trenches in front of Serre	21/10/1916	23/10/1916
War Diary	Warnimont Wood	24/10/1916	30/10/1916
War Diary	The Dell	30/10/1916	31/10/1916
Heading	War Diary. 13th Bn York & Lanc. Regt. 31st Division November 1916 Vol 9		
War Diary	The Dell	01/11/1916	03/11/1916
War Diary	Trenches	04/11/1916	07/11/1916
War Diary	Rossignol Farm	07/11/1916	09/11/1916
War Diary	Warnimont Wood	10/11/1916	11/11/1916
War Diary	Sailly	12/11/1916	12/11/1916
War Diary	Trenches	13/11/1916	13/11/1916
War Diary	The Dell	14/11/1916	16/11/1916
War Diary	Trenches	18/11/1916	22/11/1916
War Diary	Sailly	23/11/1916	27/11/1916
War Diary	Trenches	28/11/1916	30/11/1916
War Diary	War Diary 13th York & Lancaster Regt 31st Division December 1916 Vol 10		
War Diary	Trenches	01/12/1916	03/12/1916
War Diary	Sailly	04/12/1916	06/12/1916
War Diary	Trenches	07/12/1916	09/12/1916
War Diary	Sailly-Dell	10/12/1916	16/12/1916
War Diary	Sailly	17/12/1916	20/12/1916
War Diary	Trenches	21/12/1916	24/12/1916
War Diary	Rossignol Farm	25/12/1916	31/12/1916
Heading	War Diary 13th York & Lancaster Regt. 31st Division January 1917 Vol XI		
War Diary	Rossignol Farm	01/01/1917	03/01/1917
War Diary	Sailly	04/01/1917	05/01/1917
War Diary	In Trenches	06/01/1917	11/01/1917
War Diary	Beauval	12/01/1917	27/01/1917
War Diary	Montrelet	28/01/1917	31/01/1917
Heading	War Diary. 13th York & Lanc Regt. 31st Division February 1917 Vol 12		
War Diary	Montrelet	01/02/1917	08/02/1917
War Diary	Terramesnil	09/02/1917	11/02/1917
War Diary	Varennes Lealvillers	12/02/1917	13/02/1917
War Diary	Mailly-Maillet	14/02/1917	27/02/1917
Heading	War Diary 13th Bn. York & Lancaster Regt. 31st Division March 1917 Vol 13		
War Diary	Coigneux Line	01/03/1917	04/03/1917
War Diary	The Dell	05/03/1917	06/03/1917
War Diary	Courcelles Line	07/03/1917	09/03/1917
War Diary	Line	10/03/1917	11/03/1917
War Diary	Courcelles	12/03/1917	18/03/1917
War Diary	Beauval	19/03/1917	19/03/1917
War Diary	Rebreuve	20/03/1917	20/03/1917
War Diary	Valhuon	21/03/1917	21/03/1917
War Diary	Cauchy A La Tour	22/03/1917	23/03/1917
War Diary	St. Hilaire	24/03/1917	24/03/1917
War Diary	Le Sart	25/03/1917	31/03/1917
Heading	War Diary. 13th Bn. York & Lanc Regt. 31st Division April 1917 Vol 14		

War Diary	Le Sart	01/04/1917	07/04/1917
War Diary	Vendin Lez. Bethune	08/04/1917	11/04/1917
War Diary	Noeux-Les. Mines	13/04/1917	14/04/1917
War Diary	Beugin	15/04/1917	28/04/1917
War Diary	Ecoivres	29/04/1917	30/04/1917
Heading	War Diary. 13th Bn York & Lanc R. 31st Division May 1917 Vol 15		
War Diary	Ecoivres	01/05/1917	01/05/1917
War Diary	Maroeuil	02/05/1917	02/05/1917
War Diary	In The Field	03/05/1917	11/05/1917
War Diary	Railway Cutting B 27 a.	12/05/1917	20/05/1917
War Diary	Maroeuil	21/05/1917	31/05/1917
Heading	War Diary. 13th Bn. York & Lanc Regt. 31st Division June 1917 Vol 16		
War Diary	Roclincourt	01/06/1917	10/06/1917
War Diary	Railway	11/06/1917	11/06/1917
War Diary	Cutting	12/06/1917	13/06/1917
War Diary	Trenches	13/06/1917	19/06/1917
War Diary	Roclincourt	20/06/1917	26/06/1917
War Diary	Trenches	26/06/1917	30/06/1917
Heading	War Diary 13th York & Lanc Regiment 31st Division July 1917 Vol 17		
War Diary	The Cutting	01/07/1917	01/07/1917
War Diary	St Balham	02/07/1917	02/07/1917
War Diary	Bray	03/07/1917	12/07/1917
War Diary	Trenches (Acheville Sector)	13/07/1917	16/07/1917
War Diary	Trenches	21/07/1917	21/07/1917
War Diary	Rest Billets (F I d 8.3)	22/07/1917	27/07/1917
War Diary		16/07/1917	20/07/1917
War Diary	Rest Billets	27/07/1917	29/07/1917
War Diary	(Ref C 1 B N.W. 1/20000) A.G	30/07/1917	31/07/1917
Heading	War Diary. 13th Bn. York & Lanc. R. 31st Division August 1917 Vol 18		
War Diary	In Trenches Near Thelus	01/08/1917	01/08/1917
War Diary	Brigade Reserve	02/08/1917	03/08/1917
War Diary	In the Line	04/08/1917	09/08/1917
War Diary	Brigade Support	10/08/1917	15/08/1917
War Diary	Neuville-St-Vaast	16/08/1917	23/08/1917
War Diary	In the Line	24/08/1917	28/08/1917
War Diary	Brigade Support	29/08/1917	29/08/1917
War Diary	Brigade Reserve	30/08/1917	31/08/1917
Heading	War Diary. 13th York & Lancaster Regt 31st Division September 1917 Vol 19		
War Diary	Thelus Caves	01/09/1917	03/09/1917
War Diary	L2 sub sector	04/09/1917	06/09/1917
War Diary	A Support	07/09/1917	10/09/1917
War Diary	L3 Sub-Sector	11/09/1917	18/09/1917
War Diary	Springvale Camp	19/09/1917	23/09/1917
War Diary	B Support	24/09/1917	29/09/1917
War Diary	A Support	30/09/1917	30/09/1917
Heading	War Diary. 13th Battn York & Lanc R. 31st Division October 1917 Vol 20		
War Diary	Red Line	01/10/1917	05/10/1917
War Diary	Front Line Acheville Sector	06/10/1917	06/10/1917
War Diary	Front Line Acheville Sector	07/10/1917	12/10/1917
War Diary	Springvale	13/10/1917	18/10/1917

War Diary	Brown Line	19/10/1917	23/10/1917
War Diary	Red Line	24/10/1917	29/10/1917
War Diary	Front Line	30/10/1917	31/10/1917
Heading	War Diary. 13th York & Lanc Regt 31st Division November 1917 Vol 21		
War Diary	In the Trenches	01/11/1917	02/11/1917
War Diary	Acheville Sector.	03/11/1917	04/11/1917
War Diary	Springvale Camp	05/11/1917	16/11/1917
War Diary	Trenches	17/11/1917	20/11/1917
War Diary	Springvale Camp	21/11/1917	26/11/1917
War Diary	Trenches	27/11/1917	30/11/1917
Heading	War Diary. 13th Battn York & Lanc Regt. 31st Division December 1917 Vol 22		
War Diary	Trenches Oppy Sector	01/12/1917	07/12/1917
War Diary	Bray	08/12/1917	18/12/1917
War Diary	Trenches Acheville Sector	19/12/1917	24/12/1917
War Diary	Cubitt Camp	25/12/1917	30/12/1917
War Diary	Trenches Acheville Sector	31/12/1917	31/12/1917
Heading	War Diary 13 York & Lancs Vol XXVI Period 1/7/18 to 28/2/18 Date 3/3/18		
War Diary	Front Line	01/01/1918	06/01/1918
War Diary	Springvale Camp	07/01/1918	18/01/1918
War Diary	Cubitt Camp	19/01/1918	31/01/1918
War Diary	Springvale Camp	01/02/1918	04/02/1918
War Diary	Ecurie	05/02/1918	28/02/1918

Woasl 2365l2

31ST DIVISION
94TH INFY BDE

13TH BN YORK & LANCS REGT

MAR 1916 – FEB 1918

To 93 BDE 31 DIV

Confidential

Original

31st Divn Part of Not (not with M.E.F.) WAR DIARY or INTELLIGENCE SUMMARY

1/3th York & Lanc. Regt.

Army Form C. 2118

(Erase heading not required.)

Instructions regarding War Diaries and Intelligence Summaries are contained in F.S. Regs., Part II. and the Staff Manual respectively. Title Pages will be prepared in manuscript.

Place	Date	Hour	Summary of Events and Information	Remarks and references to Appendices
KANTARA	1.3.16	6.30 a.m.	Reveille. C-D Coys paraded at 6.30 a.m. for Rifle practice at Ranges made by the Battalion six miles N.E. of KANTARA. Ten rounds per man were fired. Practices (Grouping) 5 rounds (Rapid.) Lieut. H. Asquith and 6 other ranks proceeded with C. Officers charge in advance.	
do	2.3.16 to 7.3.16	6.0 a.m.	Reveille. Daily Routine.	
do	8.3.16	3.45 a.m.	Reveille. Tents struck at 5.0 a.m. Camp thoroughly cleaned before. Battalion marched out at 6.30 a.m. for KANTARA station en route for PORT SAID. By train due at 6.45 a.m. Left KANTARA station at 8.30 a.m. and arrived at PORT SAID at 10.30 a.m. Train unloaded and all baggage conveyed to Camp by 12 noon. Camp in a very dirty condition and rest of day occupied in cleaning of same.	

WAR DIARY
or
INTELLIGENCE SUMMARY

(Erase heading not required.)

Army Form C. 2118

Original

Place	Date	Hour	Summary of Events and Information	Remarks and references to Appendices
PORT SAID	9/3/16	6.30am	Reveille - Daily routine - Physical Drill and Bathing Parades	H.S.
ditto	10/3/16	6.30am	Reveille - Daily routine. Physical Drill and Bathing Parades	H.S.
ditto	11/3/16	6.30am	Reveille - Preparations made for embarking on the MEGANTIC en route for 'MARSEILLES' at 2.0.p.m. BATTALION marched out of camp at 12-30 NOON, N°S 28 officers and 920 other ranks + 10 attached. H.M.T. MEGANTIC sailed out of PORT SAID harbour at 7-30-p.m. Lt Col E.E.WILFORD, 13th Y+L Regt O.C.Troops	H.S.
H.M.T MEGANTIC	12/3/16		At Sea. Weather good.	H.S.
ditto	13/3/16		At Sea. Weather good.	H.S.

Original

WAR DIARY
or
INTELLIGENCE SUMMARY
(Erase heading not required.)

Army Form C. 2118

Instructions regarding War Diaries and Intelligence Summaries are contained in F.S. Regs., Part II. and the Staff Manual respectively. Title Pages will be prepared in manuscript.

Place	Date	Hour	Summary of Events and Information	Remarks and references to Appendices
H.M.T MEGANTIC	14/3/16		At Sea. Weather good. At 9.10.a.m. submarine reported at a distance of 1000 ft. The ship was charged at the divergence of periscope, but result not known. Anchored outside MALTA harbour for orders, and the presence of the submarine in the vicinity reported there. Off CAPE BON at 11.30.p.m.	A/S
ditto	15/3/16		At Sea. Weather good. Sighted S.W. Coast SARDINIA early. Continued in ordinary direction.	A/S
ditto.	16/3/16		Arrived at MARSEILLES, and anchored in harbour at 9.a.m. Anchored all day.	A/S
ditto	17/3/16 and 18/3/16		Breakfast on board MEGANTIC at 5.a.m. Disembarked at 9.a.m. and proceeded by route march to Station Point. 2. Battalion entrained alongside with Yorks and Regt and left Point 2. Station enroute for PONTREMY, via TARASCON. ORANGE. LYONS. DIJON. PARIS.	A/S

1875 Wt. W593/826 1,000,000 4/15 J.B.C. & A. A.D.S.S./Forms/C. 2118.

Original

Army Form C. 2118

WAR DIARY
or
INTELLIGENCE SUMMARY
(Erase heading not required.)

Instructions regarding War Diaries and Intelligence Summaries are contained in F.S. Regs., Part II. and the Staff Manual respectively. Title Pages will be prepared in manuscript.

Place	Date	Hour	Summary of Events and Information	Remarks and references to Appendices
RAILWAY TRAIN	19/3/16		Arrived at PONT REMY Station at 1·45 a.m. and train unloaded. Ammunition and baggage taken by Motor Transport. Battalion proceeded by route march to DOUDELAINVILLE a distance of 16 kilometres. Arrived at 6·30 p.m. and Battalion billeted in village.	
DOUDELAIN-VILLE	20/3/16 to 23/3/16	6.A.M.	General Routine. First 50 S.H.P.P. + 60 other ranks proceeded to MAREIUX on working party. Motor Bus.	
do.	24/3/16	6.A.M.	General Routine. Heavy Snowfall. Order from G.H.Q. to proceed on route to FONTAINE-SUR-SOMME.	
do.	25/3/16	6.A.M.	Reveille. Breakfast 6.30 A.M. March out at 9 A.M. enroute for FONTAINE-SUR-SOMME, via FRUCOURT-BAILLEUL. Arrived there at 1·30 p.m. (8 miles). Billeted for night.	
FONTAINE-SUR-SOMME	26/3/16	5·30 A.M.	Reveille. March out 8.A.M. to CANAPLES, via ETOILE and FLIXECOURT. Distance 17 miles. Arrived 5·30 p.m. and billeted for night. Cooper and and many sore feet, accounted for by cophews owing to march and wearing to boots whilst on board ship. Six failed to complete march and were sent to FIELD CLEARING STATION.	
		11·30 a.m.	Capt. SMITH, proceeded to Fourth Army Infantry School, FLIXECOURT, for short course of Instruction.	

Original

WAR DIARY
or
INTELLIGENCE SUMMARY
(Erase heading not required.)

Army Form C. 2118

Place	Date	Hour	Summary of Events and Information	Remarks and references to Appendices
CANAPLES.	27/3/16	6am	Breakfast.	
		8am	Marched to BEAUVAL via BONNEVILLE & VAL AVIR.	
		11.45am	Arrived BEAUVAL. Billeted for night — Route Fair.	
		9am	10 Officers (Capt WILKINSON, Capt FIRTH, LIEUTS. HUDSON, HEPTONSTALL, MALEHAM, Lee Cpl. HARROP, BRAITHWAITE, HUGGARD, ASQUITH, HIGINS and 40 other ranks, proceeded by motor Bus for instruction in trenches with various units.	WD
BEAUVAL	28/3/16	7am	Breakfast.	
		11am	Marched to MAILLY MAILLET via BEAUQUESNE, MARIEUX, LOUVENCOURT, BERTRANCOURT, BEAUSSART.	
		5.30pm	Arrived on outskirts of FORCEVILLE. Halted, had tea + resumed march at dusk.	
		7.25pm	Arrived MAILLY MAILLET. 26 other ranks having fallen out en route or left at DOUDELAINVILLE. Ohio compared very favourably with other Battalions of the 31st Division. The Medical Officer puts this down to their being in Egypt & on board ship. Battalion billeted in the town, the Billets were very fair on account of God feet.	WD

1875 Wt. W593/826 1,000,000 4/15 J.B.C. & A. A.D.S.S./Forms/C. 2118.

Army Form C. 2118

Original

WAR DIARY
or
INTELLIGENCE SUMMARY
(Erase heading not required.)

Instructions regarding War Diaries and Intelligence Summaries are contained in F.S. Regs., Part II. and the Staff Manual respectively. Title Pages will be prepared in manuscript.

Place	Date	Hour	Summary of Events and Information	Remarks and references to Appendices
MAILLY MAILLET	29/3/16	7am	Breakfast. The Battalion is to be employed in covering in the mining operations now going on on the front of the 31st Division is about to take over. - The work is considered to be heavy. - Three shifts of 100 men each are required every 24 hours. The Battalion will relieve 2 Battalions (approximate strength of one ordinary Battalion) of the 49th Division, at present employed on the work. The mine is situate in the Redan, about one & a half miles N.E. of the mine is situate in the now fire trench + is manned by MAILLEY MAILLET, on the now fire trench + is manned by the R.I.R. Three Officers. (Capt NORMANSELL Lts BUTTERLEY and COOKE are detailed to be responsible to the Tunnelling O. R.E. that all dirt is removed from the "SAP")	
do	"	2-30 pm	One Officer + 100 other ranks detailed from 'A'Coy for working party to report at mine head at 4 pm	
do	"	3 30 pm	No. 13/59 Col. J Bennett included in party for instruction in the trench on the 17th & most slightly wounded by shrapnel in the back of left shoulder.	M.L.

WAR DIARY or INTELLIGENCE SUMMARY

Army Form C. 2118

Original

Place	Date	Hour	Summary of Events and Information	Remarks and references to Appendices
MAILLY MAILLET	30/3/16	-	Routine Duties.	WS
do	31/3/16	-	General Routine 10 Officers & 40 Ranks detailed at CANAPLES re-joined Unit.	WS

W S Lt. Colonel.
Commandg 13th York Lanc Regt

Army Form C. 2118

WAR DIARY
or
INTELLIGENCE SUMMARY

(Erase heading not required.) 13th YORK AND LANCASTER REGT

vol 2

Place	Date	Hour	Summary of Events and Information	Remarks and references to Appendices
MAILLY MAILLET	Opl 1st to Opl 5	—	Daily Routine	do
do	Opl 6th	—	Daily Routine. At 9pm the enemy heavily shelled the right and centre of the corps front line and communication trenches, enemy shelling lasted about 90 minutes and he used gas shells. Casualties - 2 men wounded by rifle grenade & shrapnel respectively.	do
do	Apl 7th	—	Daily routine. Casualties nil.	do
do	Apl 8th	—	Daily routine. Casualties - 1 killed - by sniper. Strength 30 Officers 945 otherranks	do
do	Apl 9th	—	Daily routine. Casualties - killed 5 men - wounded 13 men + 2 Officers. (CAPT. N.W. STREAT & LIEUT. G. ASQUITH) wounded.	do
do	Apl 10th	—	Daily routine. Casualties - nil -	do
do	Apl 11th	—	Daily routine. Casualties - 1 man wounded	do

Army Form C. 2118

WAR DIARY
or
INTELLIGENCE SUMMARY
(Erase heading not required.)

13TH YORK AND LANCASTER REGT

Place	Date 1916	Hour	Summary of Events and Information	Remarks and references to Appendices
MAILLY MAILLET	apl 12th		Daily routine - Casualties - nil -	SM
do	apl 13th		Daily routine - Casualties 1 man wounded	SM
do	apl 14th		Daily routine - Casualties - 4 men gassed in mine	SM
do	apl 15th		Daily routine - Casualties - nil - Strength 28 Officers 933 other ranks	SM
do	apl 16th		Daily routine - Casualties - nil -	SM
do	apl 17th		Daily routine - Casualties - nil - Draft of men arrived - 40 - Strength 28 Officers 973 other ranks.	SM
do	apl 18th		Daily routine - Casualties - nil - A Patrol went out from N⁰ 3 Post in front of N⁰ 1 Mine, REDAN, at 8.25 pm (3 other ranks with Lieut F.T. COOPER) pushed out of large crater had been put in a style of defence, and to find a suitable spot for patrol to lie in wait for enemy patrols who might come up to the crater. Lieut COOPER & patrol returned at 9.20 pm reported that mine needed repairing at A (see map attached to two reports) a suitable spot to patrol laying at B. The crater is about 100 feet dia × 20 ft deep it had not been put in a style of defence. They saw 4 Germans on one side of crater. See Lieut COOPER's report of this night.	SM

Army Form C. 2118

WAR DIARY
or
INTELLIGENCE SUMMARY
13TH YORK AND LANCASTER REGT
(Erase heading not required.)

Place	Date 1916	Hour	Summary of Events and Information	Remarks and references to Appendices
MAILLY MAILLET	Apl 19		Daily routine - Casualties - nil -	LM
do	Apl 20		Daily routine - Casualties - nil -	LM
do	Apl 21st		Daily routine - Casualties - nil -	LM
do	Apl 22nd		Daily routine - Casualties - nil - Commenced working parties at John Tunnel, Mark Tunnel, Eczema Tunnel, Grey Tunnel, Bleneau Tunnel. Strength 28 Officers 973 Other ranks (including attached)	LM
do	Apl 23rd		Daily routine - Casualties - nil - "Draft arrived of 5 Officers + 19 men Strength 33 Officers 992 Other ranks	LM
do	Apl 24th		Daily routine - Casualties - nil -	LM
do	Apl 25th		Daily routine - Casualties - nil -	LM
do	Apl 26th		Daily routine - Casualties - nil -	LM

Army-Form C. 2118

WAR DIARY
or
INTELLIGENCE SUMMARY
(Erase heading not required.)

13TH YORK & LANCASTER REGT

Instructions regarding War Diaries and Intelligence Summaries are contained in F.S. Regs., Part II. and the Staff Manual respectively. Title Pages will be prepared in manuscript.

Place	Date 1916	Hour	Summary of Events and Information	Remarks and references to Appendices
Morally Mullet	April 27		Daily routine - Casualties- one wounded by shell fire.	SM
do	28th		do Casualties- one wounded by rifle fire. [Lt Cooper & Lt Malehant took a patrol out from No 3 observation post at REDAN at 9-0 p.m., after being out some time the enemy machine gun opened fire being impossible to advance, they returned at 12-0 p.m.	SM
do	29		do Casualties - nil - Bombardment of enemy started by our artillery at 11-30 p.m which lasted until 1 am and was very heavy while it lasted	SM
do	April 30		do - Casualties - one wounded by sniper Strength 33 officers 989 other ranks	SM

P. Rafford Lt Col.
13 Y & L.

Army Form C. 2118

WAR DIARY
or
INTELLIGENCE SUMMARY 13TH YORK AND LANCASTER REGT
(Erase heading not required.)

Vol 3
XXXI

Instructions regarding War Diaries and Intelligence Summaries are contained in F. S. Regs., Part II. and the Staff Manual respectively. Title Pages will be prepared in manuscript.

Place	Date 1916	Hour	Summary of Events and Information	Remarks and references to Appendices
Mailly Maillet	May 1st		Daily routine – casualties nil –	Lm
do	2nd		do	Lm
do	3rd		do	Lm
do	4th		do	Lm
do	5th		do Commenced working at Rees & Delaney mines	Lm
do	6th		do – Casualties – one killed by sniper at No. 3 post strength officers 32 other ranks 984.	Lm
do	7th		do – Casualties – one wounded. Draft arrived 1 Officer 20 men	Lm
do	8th		do – Casualties – one wounded	Lm

1875 Wt. W593/826 1,000,000 4/15 J.B.C. & A. A.D.S.S./Forms/C. 2118.

Army Form C.-2118

WAR DIARY
or
INTELLIGENCE SUMMARY
(Erase heading not required.)

13TH YORK AND LANCASTER REGT

Place	Date	Hour	Summary of Events and Information	Remarks and references to Appendices
Mailly Maillet 1916	May 9th		Daily routine - Casualties - nil	SM
"	10th		do Casualties - nil	SM
"	11th		do Casualties - nil	SM
"	12th		do Casualties one man	SM
"	13th		do wounded one man	SM
"	14th		do Casualties - nil	SM
"	14th		do Casualties, one killed by shell fire over billets, they shelled below A Coy billets all morning searching for batteries. Strength 30 officers, O. Ranks 1003.	SM
"	15th		do Casualties - nil -	SM
"	16th		do Casualties - nil -	SM

Army Form C. 2118

WAR DIARY
or
INTELLIGENCE SUMMARY
(Erase heading not required.)

13TH YORK & LANCASTER REGT

Instructions regarding War Diaries and Intelligence Summaries are contained in F.S. Regs., Part II. and the Staff Manual respectively. Title Pages will be prepared in manuscript.

Place	Date 1916	Hour	Summary of Events and Information	Remarks and references to Appendices
Maily Maillet	May 17th		Daily routine — Casualties — one killed by gas, caused by Germans blowing a mine at REDAN about midnight	S/w
"	18th		do — Casualties — nil —	S/w
"	19th		do — Casualties — nil —	S/w
"	20th		do — Casualties — 1 killed & 2 wounded	S/w
"	21st		do — Casualties — nil — Strength Officers 30 other ranks 996	S/w
"	22nd		do — Casualties — one Officer wounded. (2nd Lt T.E. WHITEHEAD)	S/w
"	23rd		do — Casualties — nil —	S/w
"	24th		do — Casualties — nil —	S/w

WAR DIARY
or
INTELLIGENCE SUMMARY

13TH YORK AND LANCASTER REGT

Army Form C. 2118

Place	Date 1916	Hour	Summary of Events and Information	Remarks and references to Appendices
Mailly Maillet	May 25th		Daily routine — Casualties, one wounded	LW
"	26th		do — Casualties, two wounded	LW
"	27th		do — Casualties, nil —	LW
"	28th		do — Casualties, one wounded. Strength Officers 29 Other ranks 990	LW
"	29th		do — Casualties, nil	LW
"	30th		do — Casualties, nil — We handed over the Observation Posts at REDAN, Nos 2, 3 & 3ᵃ at 6.0 a.m. this morning.	LW

Army Form C. 2118

WAR DIARY
or
INTELLIGENCE SUMMARY

(Erase heading not required.)

13TH YORK AND LANCASTER REGT

Instructions regarding War Diaries and Intelligence Summaries are contained in F. S. Regs., Part II. and the Staff Manual respectively. Title Pages will be prepared in manuscript.

Place	Date	Hour	Summary of Events and Information	Remarks and references to Appendices
MAILLY MAILLET	May 1916		Daily routine. Casualties, one O.R. wounded. Officers: 28. Strength- Other ranks: 989.	

J.M. Knowlton

XXXI

Original from
Vol VI
13 Yorks & Lancs
Vol II

WAR DIARY
or
INTELLIGENCE SUMMARY
(Erase heading not required.)

Army Form C. 2118

13 York & Lanc. R.

Instructions regarding War Diaries and Intelligence Summaries are contained in F.S. Regs., Part II. and the Staff Manual respectively. Title Pages will be prepared in manuscript.

Place	Date	Hour	Summary of Events and Information	Remarks and references to Appendices
MAILLY MAILLET	June 1st to June 3rd		Daily Routine. Casualties "NIL" Strength: Officers 28 O.R. 988	
do.	June 4th to June 10th		Daily Routine. Casualties "NIL" Draft of 2 Officers and 71 O.R. arrived June 8th Strength = Officers 30 O.R. 1059	
do.	June 10th to June 17th		Daily Routine. Casualties = Killed 3. O.R. Wounded 7. O.R. Draft of 2 officers arrived June 16/16. Strength = Officers 32 O.R. 1049	
do.	June 18th to June 24th		Daily Routine. Casualties = Killed 3.O.R. Wounded = 11.O.R. Draft of 5 officers arrived June 20/16. Warnimont under MAJOR RIALL. June 22nd. Advance party proceeded to WARNIMONT WOOD. left MAILLY MAILLET 2 p.m. arrived WARNIMONT WOOD. AUTHIE at. June 23rd. Battalion moved to WARNIMONT WOOD. AUTHIE. Main body left MAILLY MAILLET at 9 a.m. arrived at WARNIMONT WOOD 13.30 noon. Rear party left MAILLY MAILLET at 2.30 p.m. arrived WARNIMONT WOOD at 5.30 p.m.	Emp Lee Early 13 Yorkshire
WARNIMONT WOOD BUS	June 24th to June 20th		Strength: Officers 38 O.R. 1003	From 24th to 29th Daily Routine. Practising attack formations.

94th Bde.
31st Div.

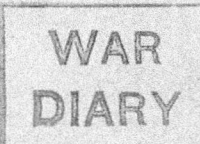

13th BATTALION

THE YORK & LANCASTER REGIMENT

JULY 1916
(30.6.16 – 31.7.16)

Confidential   Vol 5

War Diary
of
13th Bn Yorkshane Regt

from
1st July to 31st July

Original

13 York-Lanc R.

Army Form C. 2118

WAR DIARY or INTELLIGENCE SUMMARY

Vol VII page 1.

(Erase heading not required.)

Place	Date 1916	Hour	Summary of Events and Information	Remarks and references to Appendices
WARNIMONT WOOD	June 30		The Battalion strength 23 Officers 698 Other Ranks under command of Lt-Colonel Wilford left BUS at 7.40 PM and marched with the rest of the 94th B.de to proceed to their Assembly Trenches North of SERRE. Transport, Details & Reinforcements left behind amounted to 10 Officers and 174 Other Ranks.	
BUS (SOMME)	July 1	5 AM	Battalion found up in Assembly Trenches ready to advance.	
		7.30 AM	Attack on German lines and village of SERRE commenced. The Battalion being Right Reserve Bn. and following in close support of the 11/E. Lanc. R. Two Platoons of A Company under Lt. Markham (clearing up party) moved in the 2nd wave of the 11/E. Lanc. R.	
		7.40 AM	B Coy under Major Guest followed then the 4th wave, with orders to advance with the 4th & German line while the remaining 2 Platoons of A Company under Capt. Guiney advanced over our trenches into our Front Line. The advance was carried out in perfect order under a terrific hostile Artillery bombardment and machine gun fire; Major Guest and all his Officers as well as those of the "clearing party" being killed or wounded before reaching the First German line. Although this advance had to be carried out under a perfect tornado of fire, all ranks advanced as steadily as if on a drill parade. Major Guest, Lt. Hepworth and three men of B Coy reached the German first line - Major Guest and the three men were killed and Lt Hepworth was wounded in the rifle but fell into shell crater when he remained till nightfall when he	

13 Yorks-lanc R.

WAR DIARY or INTELLIGENCE SUMMARY

Army Form C. 2118

Vol VII. page 2.

Place	Date 1916	Hour	Summary of Events and Information	Remarks and references to Appendices
Trenches	July 1st	9 AM	managed to crawl back to our lines with information as to what had occurred. Orders were received for C & B Company (Capt Currin) and D Company (Capt Smith) to advance & to hold the 1st & 2nd German lines respectively, in support to our first 4 waves, who were then thought to have succeeded in reaching the German 4th & 2nd line. While these two companies were moving forward they were stopped by verbal orders from the Brigadier (who has since been informed) that all our preceding waves had been decimated and had consequently not reached their objective. C & D Companies were then ordered to reinforce to MONK TRENCH and Lt-Colonel Wilford was ordered to collect what men he could of our units and organise the defence of this trench as our second line as a German counter-attack was feared.	
		11 AM	The situation at 11 AM was as follows :— A few men of A Company under Captain Surrey assisted by stragglers from other units were holding our original front line trench which has been practically levelled & the general line C & D Companies and small parties of other units were holding MONK TRENCH on a second line, the 92nd Brigade which has been in Divisional Reserve in SACKVILLE STREET and HITTITE TRENCH having just received orders to withdraw from the line into Corps Reserve	

Original

13 Woktadene M.

Army Form C. 2118

WAR DIARY
or
INTELLIGENCE SUMMARY

Vol VIII page 3

(Erase heading not required.)

Place	Date 1916	Hour	Summary of Events and Information	Remarks and references to Appendices
Trenches	July 1st		All afternoon and evening our trenches were subjected to a very heavy bombardment with heavy H.E. Shrapnel which ceased at dark.	
		5 PM	C Company was sent to relieve the survivors of A Company who had been holding our front line and they were withdrawn to MONK TRENCH. The available strength of the Battalion at this time was about 250 all ranks. The night was spent in collecting wounded (dead) within our line and from NO MANS LAND, and in repairing our much battered trenches and consolidating our position. Captain Curvin and volunteers from C Company did splendid work in rescuing wounded from NO MANS LAND under continual fire. Several wounded & unwounded managed to return from NO MANS LAND under cover of darkness from shell craters in which they had been hiding. Reinforcements consisting of 5 Officers and 45 men arrived from those left behind at BUS. The day & night was spent in repairing our trenches, and clearing the battlefield, bringing in dead & wounded and burying the dead.	
	2nd			
	3rd		Similar to the 2nd.	
	4th		Heavy Thunder storms all day much interfered the work of repairing the trenches.	

13 York & Lanc R.

Original

WAR DIARY
INTELLIGENCE SUMMARY Vol VII page 4

Army Form C. 2118

Place	Date July	Hour	Summary of Events and Information	Remarks and references to Appendices
TRENCHES	4th		The Battalion was relieved in the evening by the 6th R.B. (Rifle Brigade) Regt and marched to LOUVENCOURT which was not reached till 5 AM the following morning.	
LOUVENCOURT	5th		The strength of the Battalion on leaving the trenches was 15 Officers and 469 Other Ranks. N.B. For list of casualties. See page 5. The day was spent in cleaning up generally and at in the afternoon the Battalion was addressed by B.Gen'l Carlo Campbell (who has returned to the Command of the 94th I.B.(?)) and Lt Gen. Sir Aylmer Hunter Weston, Commanding the VIII Corps. Both of these Generals congratulated the Battalion on its fine performance during the attack and afterwards in clearing the battle field.	
	6th		The 94th Bde marched from LOUVENCOURT to GEZAINCOURT (11 miles)	
GEZAINCOURT	7th		Rested at GEZAINCOURT	
on the march	8th		Left GEZAINCOURT at 2 PM and marched to FREVENT (12 miles) and returned at 7.30 PM	
	9th		Arrived STEENBECQUE at 4.30 AM and marched to CALONNE-SUR-LA-LYS (1st Army Area) about (11 miles) and went into billets.	

13 Yorkshires.

(Original)

WAR DIARY or **INTELLIGENCE SUMMARY**   Vol VII. Page 5.

Army Form C. 2118

(Erase heading not required.)

Place	Date 1916	Hour	Summary of Events and Information	Remarks and references to Appendices
CALONNE SUR LA LYS	July 2nd	10—	Marched to LE SART (5 miles) and went into fixed billets as there was not sufficient accommodation in those at CALONNE.	
LE SART			At 4 P.M. Lt Col Wauton O'Gowan (commanding 31st Bn) addressed the Bn's and congratulated them on their part in the attack, and subsequent times. The Battalion's casualties during the attack on the 1st July and whilst in the trenches on the 2-3-4th were as follows:— Officers — Killed 6. wounded 6. Total Officer Casualties = 12. Other Ranks — " 40 " 183. Missing 51. Total Other Ranks Casualties = 274. Total Casualties of all ranks = 286. The following Officers were killed Major T.H. Guest — Captains G de V Smith and E.H. Frith — L/Cpl A/Lieutenant H. Dent and 2nd Lt. S. Maleham and S.O. Sharp. The following were wounded:— Lts. R.A. Heftmstall. J.J. Cooke, A.P. Hunter and 2nd Lts. A.W. Knowles A.S. Braithwaite and S. Price.	

13 York & Lancs

WAR DIARY or INTELLIGENCE SUMMARY

VOL VII. page 6.

Army Form C. 2118

Place	Date 1916	Hour	Summary of Events and Information	Remarks and references to Appendices
LE SART	July 10 to 14		Resting.	
VIELLE CHAPELLE	July 14	9.30 PM	left LE SART and marched to VIELLE CHAPELLE and went into billets.	
Trenches	15	4 PM	Took over trenches in NEUVE CHAPELLE sector from 2/8 Royal Warwick R. 14th B⁺ of York & Lanc R being on our left and 17/K.R.R.s on our right.	
"	21		Sector was shelled by a 8.2" gun most of day but little material damage and few casualties. Caused thereby though 110 shells were counted. B⁺ H⁺ Q⁺ were also shelled by 5.9 and were consequently moved further back to CURZON REDOUBT	
"	24	4 PM	14/York & Lanc R took over our trenches and B⁺ H⁺ Q⁺ and we "side tracked" to the right, being established a from VINE ST to OXFORD ST, and taking over from 11/R. Sussex R and 14/Hants R, New H⁺ Q⁺ being formed at LANSDOWNE POST. A Composite Company from 11/E. Lanc. R. (94 I.B.) were attached for duty and took over our portion of the line from VINE ST to PLUM ST. 92 I.B. being on our right	

Original

13 York & Lanc. R.

Army Form C. 2118

WAR DIARY
or
INTELLIGENCE SUMMARY

VOL VII Page 7

(Erase heading not required.)

Instructions regarding War Diaries and Intelligence Summaries are contained in F.S. Regs., Part II. and the Staff Manual respectively. Title Pages will be prepared in manuscript.

Place	Date 1916	Hour	Summary of Events and Information	Remarks and references to Appendices
Trenches	25		Front line Trenches bombarded by minenwerfer both morning & evening & by 5.9. HE at intervals throughout [opened in rear of front line]. The day but few casualties were caused (though though the front line was a good deal damaged).	
"	26		do	
VIELLE CHAPELLE	27	4PM	Relieved by 18/W. York. R. (93 I.B.) and marched to VIELLE CHAPELLE to billets. Ordered to stand haram from 10.30 PM till 4 AM 28/7/16 owing to Germans having raided our front line, but were not repulsed. During our tour of duty in the Trenches the Bn. incurred the following casualties: Capt Normansell & 2/Lt Harris wounded - Other ranks 6 killed & 40 wounded.	
"	29		A party of 2 Officers and 60 O.R. (A Coy.) attached to 93 I.B. as a "Reserve".	
"	31		Capt E.H. Gurney posted to 12/York & Lanc. R. with orders to take over command of that Bn.	

[signature] Major
C'mdg 13 York & Lanc R.

Confidential   Vol #216

War Diary
of
13th (S) Yorkshire Regt.

Aug 1916.

Original

13th York & Lancs Rgt

WAR DIARY
or
INTELLIGENCE SUMMARY
(Erase heading not required.)

Army Form C. 2118

Vol VIII Page I

Place	Date 1916	Hour	Summary of Events and Information	Remarks and references to Appendices
VIEILLE CHAPELLE	AUG 1 to AUG 4th		Resting. Rest Billets.	
TRENCHES NEUVE CHAPELLE SECTOR	Aug 4th	9.30 PM	Left VIEILLE CHAPELLE & took over trenches in NEUVE CHAPELLE Sector. A & D Coys were attached to the 14th York & Lancs to assist. Held the line from SIGN POST LANE to OXFORD ST. C Coy was attached to the composite Bn of the 11th East Lancs & 12th York & Lancs to assist held the line from OXFORD ST to VINE ST = B Coy. Held various posts West of the line. Bn Hd Qrs were at CROIX BARBÉE in the RUE DU PUITS.	
NEUVE CHAPELLE SECTOR	Aug 7th Aug 8th	9.30 AM	C Coy were relieved & went into Billets at CROIX BARBÉE. Took over Front Line trenches from 14th York & Lancs + 12th York & Lancs from CHURCH RD to PIONEER ST. Bn Hd Qrs were at CURZON POST. A. B. & C Coys in the Front Line + D Coy in support in B. LINE. The 11th East Lancs were on our Right & the 2/4th Royal Warwicks on our Left. Enemy was fairly quiet during this period although there was	

1875 Wt. W 593/826 1,000,000 4/15 J.B.C. & A. A.D.S.S./Forms/C. 2118.

Original.

13th Yorks Lanc Rgt

WAR DIARY or **INTELLIGENCE SUMMARY**

Army Form C. 2118

Vol VIII Page 2

Place	Date	Hour	Summary of Events and Information	Remarks and references to Appendices
TRENCHES	AUG 9th		considerable artillery activity at times. Our total casualties during the period here — 2nd Lt. England (wounded & since attached 14th York & Lancs) 22nd Lt. Dixon (wounded) Other Ranks, 4 killed	
VIEILLE CHAPELLE	Aug 18th	5 PM	10 wounded. CAPT R.W. CURRIN was awarded the D.S.O. on the 7th inst. for gallantry displayed during the attack on SERRE (Battle of the Somme). Relieved by the 2/5th Gloucesters & marched into rest billets at VIEILLE CHAPELLE. 100 men were attached to the 92nd Brigade at RICHEBOURG ST VAAST for work in the trenches	
A:	Aug 25th		Remaining Rest Billets.	
Detained Posts	Aug 28th	Noon	Left VIEILLE CHAPELLE & took over trenches from the 4th & 5th Gloucesters & the 7th & 8th Worcesters. A & C Coys were in close reserve. The Bn HQ at MAISON RASEE at PENIN MARIAGE POST. Battalion Headquarters	
NEUVE CHAPELLE SECTOR	Aug 31st	6 PM	The following Officers joined the Battalion on this date — Captain F.W. L. Field, Capt A.E. Thorn, Lec Lt J. Teasdale, Lee Lt J.M. Wise & Lee Lt W.R.W. Knights (Ration) Strength of Battalion 24 Officers 470 Other Ranks C.O. Lt-Colonel C.P.B. Riall (East Yorkshire Regt)	A/Vielle de Cie 13th York & Lanc Regt Only

1875. Wt. W593/826 1,000,000 4/15 J.B.C. & A. A.D.S.S./Forms/C. 2118.

Confidential   Vol III

War Diary.

13th York & Lancaster Regt.   31st Division

September 1916.

Army Form C. 2118

WAR DIARY or INTELLIGENCE SUMMARY

(Erase heading not required.)

Original   VOL IX Page I   13 York & Lancaster Regt

Place	Date	Hour	Summary of Events and Information	Remarks and references to Appendices
DEFENDED POSTS NEUVE CHAPELLE SECTOR	Sept 2nd	9 AM	Handed over posts to 11TH EAST LANCS. Bt Coys in billets at PENIN MARIAGE during night of 2nd/3rd. Lieut C.B. DIXON joined the Battalion on this date.	L.E. Hoffman a.d.c.
	Sept 3rd	9 AM	Left PENIN MARIAGE & took over front line trenches from SIGNPOST LANE to FIFTEENTH ST from the 2/0TH WORCESTERS & 12TH YORK & LANCS. A.B. & D Coys were in the front line & a Coy in support in 3 lines. Bn HdQrs were at CURZON POST. Lt-Col RIALL went on leave this day. 12TH YORK & LANCS were on our right & the 2/6 TH GLOUCESTERS on our left. Enemy heavy artillery was very active during the period. On 10th inst in the early hours of the morning the 12th YORK & LANCS on our right carried out a successful raid. Casualties during the period amounted to - Killed 1 (2 Lt F.M. WISE) wounded 10 OR, & accidentally wounded 1 (Sgt NEWTON)	
TRENCHES				
LESTREM	Sept 11th	10 AM	Left trenches & marched to billets at LESTREM Relieved in the line by 18TH D.L.I. 93RD BDE. Lt-Col RIALL returned from leave this day. 2nd Lieut Q. Holman & 2/o Lt E. PARKER joined the Battalion on this date both having been posted from the SOUTH STAFFORDSHIRE REGT.	
	Sept 13th		Resting & finding working parties in the line. See Reports T. STIRRUP & C. KIRK joined the Battalion this day	

Army Form C. 2118

WAR DIARY
or
INTELLIGENCE SUMMARY

(Erase heading not required.)

Original   VOL IX Page 2
3/6 York and Lancaster Regt

Place	Date	Hour	Summary of Events and Information	Remarks and references to Appendices
LESTREM	Sept 13th		Resting	
	Sept 15th			H. Hoffmonted
DEFENDED POSTS FESTUBERT SECTOR	Sept 16th	10.30 AM	Left LESTREM & moved into Festubert Sector. Motor lorries were used to move the Battalion. A Coy were attached to the 11th East Lancs & were in the line in the right sub sector & B Coy were attached to the 12th York & Lancs & were in the line in the left sub sector. C Coy held posts in & around FESTUBERT - East of the Rue de FESTUBERT & D Coy held various posts in the VILLAGE LINE. Bn = D Coy. HR. Qrs were in RUE EPINETTE.	
Trenches	Sept 23rd		Lt. Col. E.C. Wilfer returned from sick leave during the afternoon & took over Command of the Battalion.	CHR
FESTUBERT Sector	Sept 24th		Took on Right Sub-Sector from 11th East Lancs. C. Company and 3 Platoons of A. Coy held Princes Island & Islands 1-9 with Coy H5 QP at GEORGE Street. D. Company and 1 Platoon of A. Company held Islands 10, 10A, 11, 12, 13, and 13A with Coy H5 QP at COVE.R.TRENCH. B. Coy were in Support on the Right in O.B.L. and 1 Coy 11th East Lancs were in support on the left in O.B.L. B'. H5 Grs in O.B.L. (A.2.C.50.55).	2/H
	Sept 25 Sept 26		Capt Irwin was evacuated sick. Lieut Dixon who evacuated sick. Enemy was very inactive, with the exception of his Machine guns and Snipers.	CHR

1875 Wt. W593/826 1,000,000 4/15 J.B.C. & A. A.D.S.S./Forms/C.2118.

WAR DIARY or INTELLIGENCE SUMMARY

Army Form C. 2118

(Erase heading not required.) Original B^n Yorks&Lancs Regt Vol. IX Page 3.

Place	Date	Hour	Summary of Events and Information	Remarks and references to Appendices
Trenches FESUBERT SECTOR	Sept 21st to 30th		Casualties during this period amounts to 1 killed, 3 wounded and 1 accidentally wounded (pte Thirkle). Strength of the Battalion on Sept 30th was 30 officers 620 other Ranks.	CH12. CH12

M J Rae
Lt. C.S. & Lt.
Commdg. 1/3 Y & L Service Regt

Confidential.

Volume 8

War Diary.

3rd Bn. York Lancaster Regt. 31st Division

October 1916.

Confidential 1/5th York Lancaster Regt Original

Army Form C. 2118

Instructions regarding War Diaries and Intelligence Summaries are contained in F.S. Regs., Part II. and the Staff Manual respectively. Title Pages will be prepared in manuscript.

WAR DIARY
INTELLIGENCE SUMMARY
(Erase heading not required.)

Vol. X. Page 1

Place	Date	Hour	Summary of Events and Information	Remarks and references to Appendices
FESTUBERT SECTOR	Oct. 1		Relieved in the trenches by the 11th East Lancs, and went into billets at LE TOURET. 2nd Lt Midwood proceeds on to ABBEVILLE on a Transport Course.	1/11/12
VENDIN-LEZ-BETHUNE	3.		The Battalion marches by Companies to VENDIN-LEZ-BETHUNE. Strength 30 officers and 619 other ranks on leaving Base but 24 officers & 501 O.Ranks present with Batt.	CHR
ROBECQ	5.		The Battalion marches by Companies to ROBECQ, billets at VENDIN-LEZ-BETHUNE being taken over by 12th B. Y.L. Regt. R.S.M. KNARTON and 4 men proceed to Base depot on recommendation of A.D.M.S.	CHR
			The Battalion was reviewed at ROBECQ by Ale 8th Kenning (?)	CHR
	8th		Marches to SARTON arriving about 12.30 A.M. on the 9th. Strength 25 officers. 539 O.Ranks. marches to BERGUETTE and entrains for DOULLENS.	CHR
SARTON.			present with Battalion.	CHR
Sarton.	11.		Major G.B. Wanhope rejoined on arrival, and took over the duties of 2 i/c in command of the 12th York and Lancaster Regt. from Major Riall	CHR
	12.		2nd Lieut. Laws admitted to hospital.	
	13.		A draft of 98. O.R. arrived, including 14 signallers.	6/11/12
	14.		A draft of 71 O.R. arrives including 8 Sgts, mostly 3rd Battalion men.	
	15.		1 officer 24. O.Ranks 717. Strength	CHR
	17.		A fine week in the area. requests by the Battalion, if to be cut about 8-10. P.M. in our new recruit trams. A number of drains	CHR

13th York & Lancs Rgt
Confidential (Original)

Army Form C. 2118

WAR DIARY
or
INTELLIGENCE SUMMARY
(Erase heading not required.)

Vol. X. Page 11.

Place	Date	Hour	Summary of Events and Information	Remarks and references to Appendices
SARTON	Oct 17		and stores were burnt and the greatest work done by the Battalion undoubtedly rewards greater tonnage being done.	C/12
	18.		The Battalion marched from SARTON at 2=30 P.M. and reached WARNIMONT WOOD at 5 P.M.	C/R
WARNIMONT WOOD.	19-20.		Training in WARNIMONT WOOD.	
Trenches in front of SERRE	21.		Left WARNIMONT WOOD and proceeded in Buses to COURCELLE. Owing to the buses only reporting at 6-30 the Batt: were 2 hours late & O.C. 76th Bde - 3rd Division to which the Battalion was attached gave orders for the Battalion to move in COURCELLE till 5 P.M. Relief complete at 10-30 P.M. B.Coy on Right and B.Coy on Left held front line. A Coy in right and C Coy on Left held Support line. B'n HQ 19'. LEGEND. Strength: Officers 20. other Ranks 603.	C/R
	23.		Relieved by 2 Companies H.L. Royal Fusiliers and 2 Companies Royal Scots. Relief complete at 1-15. A.M. Slight shelling during Relief. Met orders at COURCELLE and enough Buses carrying HQ? and two Companies back to WARNIMONT WOOD. Casualties during tour of duty & during relief. Died of wounds 1 other Ranks. Wounded 5 other Ranks. + 4 of C.N.R. 2-9 M.M.M. 29 Officers. 774 other Ranks.	A/12
			Strength of Batt: –	
WARNIMONT WOOD	24. 25. 26.		Weather wet. 2/Lieut WILLIAMS evacuated sick. Roads & carrying party. 4 other ranks wounds. Working parties carrying T.M. Ammunition. 5 wounded. Strength Officers 27. O.R. 765-	H/R
"	27 to 30.		Working parties. Moves to the DELL (H.Q.B.T.17.V.4.4) relieving 16th West Yorks	C/12

Confidential Original

10th York & Lancaster Rgt.

Army Form C. 2118

WAR DIARY
INTELLIGENCE SUMMARY

(Erase heading not required.)

Vol. X Page III

Instructions regarding War Diaries and Intelligence Summaries are contained in F. S. Regs., Part II. and the Staff Manual respectively. Title Pages will be prepared in manuscript.

Place	Date	Hour	Summary of Events and Information	Remarks and references to Appendices
The DELL	30.		Providing working parties (every available man) for clearing out revetting positions of NAIRNE, CABER and JONES. Strength of Battalion officers 27. O.Ranks 756.	SH/2/
"	31.		1-11-16.	A. M. Floyd Capt. 13 Y&L

Confidential

Volume XI

Vol 9

War Diary.

13th Bn York Lanc. Regt   31st Division

November 1916.

Original 18th York & Lanc Rgt. Confidential

Army Form C. 2118

WAR DIARY
or
INTELLIGENCE SUMMARY

(Erase heading not required.) Vol. XI. Page 1.

Place	Date	Hour	Summary of Events and Information	Remarks and references to Appendices
The DELL	Nov 1st to 3rd		Providing working parties for the trenches. Strength officers 27, O.Ranks 755. One O.Rank wounded.	A112
TRENCHES	4.	1.15 pm	Took over trenches (JOHN.COPSE to JENA) from the 11th East Lancs. Relief complete at 1.15 p.m. A and C Companies in front line, B and D in support. H.Qrs. in GETORIX. Casualties 7. O.Ranks wounded.	A112
"	5.		Draft 7. O.Ranks arrives. Casualties nil.	
"	6. to 7.		A successful raid was carried out on the night 6/7. White cover of an intense bombardment a raiding party consisting of 2nd Lieuts Barnes and Knight and 57. O.Ranks entered the enemy's trenches at K.17.d.12.12. Four (4) prisoners (two wounded) were captured and the dugouts filled up with bombs. The extent of the enemy's casualties were estimated at 30. Killed - while our own losses were only 5. O.Ranks wounded. Telegrams of congratulations were received from G.O.C. XIII Corps, G.O.C. 31st Division, G.O.C. 92nd Brigade & Bgde Commd. 2nd Lieuts Barnes and 2nd Lieut Knight awarded the Military Cross & 2 ranks the Military Medal.	A112
ROSSIGNOL FARM	7.		Relieved by 16th West Yorks (Relief complete at 1.15 PM) and proceed to ROSSIGNOL FARM	412
"	8.		Draft 6. O.Ranks arrives.	
"	9.		Providing working parties.	
"	10.		Providing working parties. Batt. ROSSIGNOL FARM at 2.30 PM and proceeds to WARNIMONT WOOD. Strength officers 26. O.Ranks wounded 11. O.Ranks. Casualties Killed 1. O.Rank wounded 11. O.Ranks.	4R
WARNIMONT WOOD	11.		In WARNIMONT WOOD	JR

Original 10th Bn. Lancaster Rgt. Confidential

Army Form C. 2118

Instructions regarding War Diaries and Intelligence Summaries are contained in F.S. Regs., Part II. and the Staff Manual respectively. Title Pages will be prepared in manuscript.

WAR DIARY or INTELLIGENCE SUMMARY

(Erase heading not required.)

Vol. XI Page 2

Place	Date	Hour	Summary of Events and Information	Remarks and references to Appendices
SAILLY	Nov. 12		Attaches to 92nd Brigade and marches to SAILLY, being in Brigade Reserve. H.Q. at J.17.b.3.3. Strength officers 18. O. Ranks 544.	CWR
Trenches	13		Battalion remains in SAILLY ready to move at 20 minutes notice. Orders were received at 3=50 PM to proceed to RAPIN and GÉTORIX via JEAN BART. and to take over the line from NAIRNE to JEAN BART. A. Coy. half CABER. C. Coy. YELLOW LINE, B. Coy. GÉTORIX and D. Coy. RAPIN. Patrols were organised to bring in wounded from that line + No. Mans Land, 3 officers and over 60. other ranks being brought in	CWR
The DELL	14		Relieved by 11th East Lancs and proceeds to the DELL. Casualties 2 killed 3 wounded. Draft of 3 officers arrives. Lieut O'SULLIVAN. 2 Lieut SPARROWS 2 Lieut TOMSHURST. Strength officers 29. O. Ranks 736. Draft 5. O. Ranks arrives.	CWR
"	16.		Relieves 11th E. Lancs. in the trenches. B. Coy Right Front, A. Coy Night Support, C. Coy Left Front, B. Coy left Support. One other rank wounded. Advance posts were wires and a piece dug to drain TENA.	CWR
Trenches	18.			
	19 to 21			CWR
	22		Relieved by 11th East Lancs. Relief complete at 2=15 PM. Proceeds to SAILLY. 1 Other rank wounded.	CWR

Original 13th York & Lanc. Bn.

Confidential.

Army Form C. 2118

WAR DIARY
or
INTELLIGENCE SUMMARY

(Erase heading not required.)

Vol XI Page 3.

Place	Date	Hour	Summary of Events and Information	Remarks and references to Appendices
SAILLY	23.		Battalion Resting.	
	24.		Working parties. CAPT. HUMPHRIES. R.A.M.C. left to join 93rd Field Ambulance, being relieved	A/R
	25.		by Capt. D.F. SKEEN.	C/12
	26.		Strength officers 29. other ranks 785.	
	27		Draft 38 other ranks arrived.	
Trenches.	28.		Relieved 11th EAST. LANCS. in the trenches. A.Coy right front, B. Right Support, C Left	
			front, D. Left Support. Strength 20 officers 749. O. Ranks.	
"	30.		2Lieut HERTON accidentally wounded in foot.	
"	30.		Two Snipers went out into NO MANS LAND and claimed to have hit six (6)	
			Germans.	

2. Dec 1915.

[signature]
Lt. Col.
Commanding
13th Bn York & Lanc.
Regt.

Confidential

Volume ~~III~~ Vol 10

War Diary

13th York Lancaster Regt.   31st Division

December 1916.

Original
Confidential

1/3th York Lancaster Regt.

WAR DIARY
or
INTELLIGENCE SUMMARY

Army Form C. 2118

Vol. XII. Page 1.

Place	Date	Hour	Summary of Events and Information	Remarks and references to Appendices
Trenches	Dec. 1st		Major Newbys left to take command of the 11th East Lancs. — 1 O.R. killed, & 2 wounded.	
	2.		1 Other Rank wounded. Strength: — 29 Officers 808 Other Ranks.	
	3.		Relieved by 11th East Lancs. Relief complete at 2–10 p.m. Proceeded to billets in SAILLY.	J.C.S.
SAILLY	4.		Daily Routine.	
	5.		Providing working parties. Draft of 26 Other Ranks arrived.	
	6.		Providing working parties. Lt. Col. E.E. Wilford evacuated sick. Capt. C.H. Robin assumed command of the Battalion.	
Trenches	7.		Relieved the 11th East Lancs. in the trenches. Relief complete at 1.40 p.m. Draft of 44 O.R. arrived, but remained with transport at COIGNEUX. Lt. G.H. Hudson rejoined from T.M.B. & was posted to A. Coy.	J.C.S.
	8.		1 O.R. killed & 4 wounded. Draft of 38 O.R. arrived & remained at COIGNEUX.	
	9.		Relieved by one company of the 11th East Lancs. and three Coys of the 13th King's Liverpool Regt. 1 O.R. wounded. Strength — 29 officers. 902 Other Ranks. Proceeded to the DELL. (SAILLY.)	
SAILLY-DELL	10.		Rest. Draft of 2 other ranks arrived.	J.C.S.
	11.		Finding working parties. Capt. F.W.L. Huck returned from Course & took over duties as 2nd in Command.	
	12.		Finding working parties.	
	13.		Providing working parties. L.C. O'Sullivan admitted to hospital.	
	14.		Finding working parties.	
	15.		Providing working parties.	
	16.		Finding working parties. Strength: — 29 Officers, 894 Other Ranks.	
SAILLY	17.		Moved to SAILLY. B & D Coys went into the trenches with A & C Coys at SAILLY.	J.C.S.
	18.		Finding working parties.	J.C.
	19.		Providing working parties. Draft of 5 O.R. arrived. 1 O.R. wounded.	
	20.		Finding working parties. "C" Coy relieved 1 Coy of "D" in the trenches. Draft of 76 O.R. arrived.	
Trenches	21.		"A" Coy went into trenches. "D" Coy took over from them. Two Coys of Stay attached. 4 O.R. wounded. 10 Germans taken prisoners.	J.C.

10th Bn York & Lancaster Regt.
Confidential
Army Form C. 2118

WAR DIARY
INTELLIGENCE SUMMARY
(Erase heading not required.)

Original

Vol. XII. Page 2.

Place	Date	Hour	Summary of Events and Information	Remarks and references to Appendices
Trenches.	Dec. 22.		Finding working parties.	
	23.	10.0 p.m.	"C" Coy under Capt. FOERS raided enemy's trenches, under cover of an intense bombardment. The raiding party consisted of Capt. FOERS & 2/Lt. MIDWOOD + 77 O.R. Point of entry was K.17.d.12.12. The party entered enemy trenches an explosion occurred, wounding 2/Lt. MIDWOOD & 7 Other Ranks. Capt. FOERS and a small party proceeded up the trench and bombed the enemy dug-out with Mills' bombs & P'grenades, the Germans refusing to come out when Capt FOERS shouted "KOMMEN SIE MIT." The party was forced to leave the trench owing to the fumes which proceeded from the burning dug-out. Capt FOERS & his small party succeeded in bringing back 2/Lt. MIDWOOD to our lines under heavy machine gun fire from the enemy. Our Casualties were 2 Officer + 8 O.R. wounded. The enemy's losses cannot be estimated but he must have suffered very heavily. Early in morning of 24th two Germans walked into our posts & were captured. They belonged to 8th Bavarian Inf. Regt. Strength :- 27 Officers + 949 Other Ranks.	Ys.
	24.		"A" Coy was relieved by "A" Coy of the 11th East Lancs: Regt. & proceeded to DELL. Capt. C.H. ROBIN proceed on leave to U.K. + Capt. F.W.L. HULK took command. 3 O.R. wounded.	Ys.
Rossignol Farm.	25.		Battalion was relieved by the 14th Y.& L. + proceeded to ROSSIGNOL FARM, COIGNEUX. (Relief complete 12-0 noon) 2/Lt. MIDWOOD died of wounds in Field Ambulance.	Ys.
	26.		Rest Day. Men had their Xmas dinners.	
	27.		Finding working parties of 10 Off. + 60 O.R. Daily Routine.	
	28.		Daily Routine. Finding small working parties.	
	29.		Finding working parties – 2 Off + 260 O.R. 2/Lt. HEPTON returned from hospital. Draft of 50 O.R. arrived.	
	30.		Daily Routine. Strength:- 26 Off. 946.O.R.	Ys.
	31.		Daily Routine.	

1st Jan. 1917.

F.W.L. Hulk.
Captain.
Comm. Og 13th 0 13th Bn York & Lanc: Regt.

Confidential.

Volume XI.

Vol XI

War Diary.

13th York Lancaster Regt. 31st Division

January 1917.

WAR DIARY or INTELLIGENCE SUMMARY

Army Form C. 2118.

13th York Lanc Rgt
Vol. XIII. Page 1.
Original

Place	Date	Hour	Summary of Events and Information	Remarks and references to Appendices
ROSSIGNOL FARM.	Jan. 1st		'A' Coy proceeded to the trenches.	
	2nd		Left ROSSIGNOL FARM & went to SAILLY. 'C' Coy went into the line.	
SAILLY.	3rd		Finding working parties. Casualties 2 killed & 1 wounded (Other Ranks).	Nil.
	4th		Finding working parties.	
	5th		Providing working parties. Major F.J. COURTENAY HOOD took over command of the Battalion.	
	6th		Relieved 12th York & Lancs: in the line. Draft of 64 O.R. arrived. Casualties & wounded. Strength 25 off. – 937 O.R.	
In TRENCHES.	7th 8th		In the trenches.	
	9th		Draft of 6 O.R. & 3 officers arrived. 2nd Lts SIDDELL – DAVIDSON – PHILLIPS.	
	10th		Casualties. 3 O.R. killed + 3 wounded.	Nil.
	11th		Relieved by 6th Wilts. Regt. Relief complete at 7-30 p.m. "Embussed" at the DELL, en route for BEAUVAL at 2.0 A.M.	
BEAUVAL.	12th		Arrived BEAUVAL. Rest Day.	
	13th		Training. Strength 28 off. – 1015 Other Ranks.	
	14th 15th 16th 17th 18th 19th		Training & Daily Routine.	
	20th		Training. Draft of 2 officers Arrived. CAPT. NORMANSELL + 2nd LT ROWLAND. Strength. 30 off. – 1005 Other Ranks.	Nil.
	21st		Draft of 3 officers arrived. CAPT. M.G. WILSON ; LIEUT. RAE , & 2nd LT. NORTH.	
	22nd		Training. Draft of 13 O.R. arrived. 2nd LT. DAVIDSON admitted to Hospital.	
	23rd 24th 25th 26th		Training + Daily Routine.	
	27th		Training. Strength. 33 Officers – 993 O.R.	

Army Form C. 2118.

13th York & Lanc Regt

Vol. XIII. Page 2.

WAR DIARY
or
INTELLIGENCE SUMMARY.

(Erase heading not required.)

Original

Place	Date	Hour	Summary of Events and Information	Remarks and references to Appendices
MONTRELET	Jan. 28th		Battalion moved to MONTRELET.	2 cos.
	29th		Hon. Lt. & Q.M. SMAILES admitted to Hospital.	
	30th 31st		Training & Daily Routine.	

2.2.17.

M Mountfoot Lieut Colonel.
Commdg. 13th York & Lancaster Regt.

Confidential.

Vol IV.

War Diary.

13th York Lanc. Regt.   31st Division

February 1917.

INTELLIGENCE SUMMARY.

13th York & Lancaster

Vol. XIV Page 1.

Place	Date FEB.	Hour	Summary of Events and Information	Remarks and references to Appendices
MONTRELET	1-7		The Battalion carries out training during the mornings and sports during the afternoons. Weather very cold. Strength of Battalion officers 33. O. Ranks 963.	CHR.
	8		Marches to TERRAMESNIL in very cold weather. Orders received to remain there till the 12th.	
TERRAMESNIL	9-11		Training continued. Lieut Huggans rejoined on the 10th and Major Currin D.S.O. and Capt Knowles on the 11th.	CHR.
VARENNES?	12.		H.Qrs and C and D. Coys marches to VARENNES and A and B under Major Currin D.S.O. to LEALVILLERS.	CHR.
LEALVILLERS	13.		Cleaning up and resting.	
MAILLY-MAILLET	14.		A and B. Companies moved to MAILLY-MAILLET-WOOD. C and D. Companies started work on Light Railway line under direction of 2"B" Canadian Railway Construction Troops.	H
	15-20		Whole Battalion working on Railways. Lt-Col Hood proceeded on leave on the 16th and Maj Currin D.S.O. assumes command of the Battalion. Strength Officers 34. O.Ranks 952. W/e	
	20-28		Working parties daily. Weather mild with a good deal of fog.	
	26		Draft 5. O. R. arrives. Strength 32 officers 947 O.Ranks.	
	27.		Capt Knowles proceeded to 5th Army School. Lieut Braithwaite reports for duty.	

1-3-17 R.W. Currin Major Commg 13th Y & L Regt

Confidential

Volume XV

VM 13

War Diary.

13th Bn. York & Lancaster Regt. 31st Division

March 1917.

Army Form C. 2118.

WAR DIARY
or
INTELLIGENCE SUMMARY.
(Erase heading not required.)

Original

Place	Date	Hour	Summary of Events and Information	Remarks and references to Appendices
	March			
COIGNEUX - Line	1st		H/s Q². B, C, and D moves to COIGNEUX, A Company to COUIN.	eH/R
	2nd		The Battalion took over the line in vicinity of ROSSIGNOL WOOD. A and B. Coys holds the wood and posts EAST and both EAST of it and took over and consolidates the GARDE STELLING from which the enemy has been driven to have previously. C. Company were in Support with the B/2 at the Crucifix and D. Coy in Reserve in old German 3rd line. Bn H⁰ Q² at K11D 60.45. Strength 3 H officers. 942. O. Ranks.	
	3-5.		Remains in the line, active patrolling and salvage work.	CH/R
	4.		Bt-Col E.E. Wilfors D.S.O. returns from sick leave and took over command of the Battalion.	eH/R
The DELL.	5.		Moves out of the line to the DELL. Heavy fall of snow.	
	6		Resting and cleaning up at the DELL	
COURCELLES	7		Moves from the DELL to COURCELLES.	
Line	9-		Moves into the line EAST and NORTH EAST of PUISIEUX, marching via MAILLY - AUCHONVILLERS - BEAUMONT-HAMEL and BEAUCOURT. Strength 33 officers 940. O ranks. C. Coy left front Coy, D Coy right front Coy. B. Coy in GUDGON Trench and A. Coy in Reserve in PUISIEUX - BEAUCOURT Road at about L.20.c. Bn H⁰Q² L.20 c.5.7.	

WAR DIARY
or
INTELLIGENCE SUMMARY.

Army Form C. 2118.

B/K York & Lanc Rgt

1 June XI. Page 2.

Place	Date	Hour	Summary of Events and Information	Remarks and references to Appendices
Lime	March 10		Capt. & T. Hannaford died of wounds received the night before. D.O. Sander wounded. Strength 33 officers. 940. other ranks.	CHR
"	11		I.O. made sallies. 4 o. ranks wounded. A wounded German of the 86th Fusilier Regt surrenders to our posts. situates at L.15.c.3.3.	CHR.
COURCELLES	12		The Battalion less 'Q' Company were relieved by the 2/4th York & Lanc. Regt at 2.0.a.m and 5 marches to COURCELLES.	CHR
"	13		Working parties started on broad gauge railway from Lucerne to Levil. A Company being relieved by 62nd Div. before the Battalion.	W.O.T.
"	14/18		Battalion on railway working parties.	W.O.T.
Bequval	19		Battalion moved to Bleuval via Louvencourt, Rauchecal & Burgneville. Strength 32 officers, 948 other Ranks.	W.O.T.
Rebreuve	20.		Capt. Berry evacuated sick. Battalion moved to Rebreuve via Sullen, & Burgneuvon.	W.O.T.
Valhuon	21.		Battalion moved to Valhuon via Frevent Hung & St. Pol.	W.O.T.
Cauchy à Tour	22.		Battalion marched to Cauchy à Tour via Pernes. Snowfell in heavy falls.	W.O.T.
"	23		Resting & cleaning up at Cauchy à to Tour.	W.O.T.
St. Hilaire	24		Battalion moved to St. Hilaire Cottes via Ferfay & Lieres.	W.O.T.

Army Form C. 2118.

WAR DIARY
or
INTELLIGENCE SUMMARY.

(Erase heading not required.) 13th York Lane Regt W XV Lines 8

Instructions regarding War Diaries and Intelligence Summaries are contained in F. S. Regs., Part II. and the Staff Manual respectively. Title pages will be prepared in manuscript.

Original

Place	Date	Hour	Summary of Events and Information	Remarks and references to Appendices
Le Sart	March 25.		Battalion marched to Le Sart via Ham en Artois & St Venant thus completing a distance of 63 miles.	CHR.
"	26.		Battalion resting at Le Sart.	CHR. 2
"	27. to 31.		Training in vicinity of LE SART - Musketry and Bombing practice, and visits to fighting area. Carried out. Strength officers 36. O.Ranks 975.	CHR.
"	30.		Lieut Tyzack evacuated to Field Ambulance.	CHR.
"	31.		Maj R.T. Currin J.S.O. left for England to attend Senior Officers course	CHR.

R M Fort
Lieut. Col.
Commanding 13th York Lanc. Regt.

Confidential

Volume XVI

Vol 14

War Diary.

13th Bn. York Lanc Regt 31st Division

April 1917

Army Form C. 2118.

WAR DIARY
or
INTELLIGENCE SUMMARY.
(Erase heading not required.)

13th York Lancaster Regt
Vol XVI Page 1

Place	Date	Hour	Summary of Events and Information	Remarks and references to Appendices
Le Quesnoy	April 1st		Training in vicinity of Lillers. Lt A.T.B. Clutts reports for duty/posted to A Coy.	
	2nd		Training in vicinity of Lillers. Musketry & Bombing.	
	3rd		Training in Musketry & Bombing, with Rifle Grenade possible also.	
	4th			
	5th		a short route march.	
	6th		General training & inspection by the C.O.	
	7th		Strength 38 Officers 989 Other ranks.	
	8th		move to VENDIN LEZ BETHUNE.	
VENDIN LEZ BETHUNE	9		General training, i.e. musketry, bombing, bayonet fighting, physical training	
"	10		Training of Grenadiers in supervision of bombs. Bombinier wants smoke Train.	
"	11		move to NOEUX-LES-MINES.	
NOEUX- LES MINES	13		Capt a. H.L. MARWOOD reports his arrival & took over the duties of 2nd in command. marches to BEUGIN via HOUDAIN.	
	14		Training at BEUGIN. 2/Lt H Ashcroft & 2/Lieut J.C. Stephenson reports for duty, & are taken on the strength 9th Battalion	

WAR DIARY
or
INTELLIGENCE SUMMARY.

Army Form C. 2118.

18th Bttn Lancaster Regt
Vol. XVI Page II

Place	Date	Hour	Summary of Events and Information	Remarks and references to Appendices
BEUGIN.	April 15 to 28		Training - Open warfare training, practices & musketry. Strength - Officers 39 - other ranks 935.	CWR. CWR
ECOIVRES	29.		marches to ECOIVRES via FREVILLERS - SAVY - AUBIGNY - FREVIN-CAPELLE and ACQ. Hot and dusty march.	CWR
"	30.		Cleaning up and resting	

A.J.K. Magnis(?) Maj to Lieut Colonel
Commanding 18th York Lancaster Regt

Confidential   Volume XVII

                                YT/15

                War Diary.

                                31st Division

13th Bn York & Lanc R.

                    May 1917.

WAR DIARY or INTELLIGENCE SUMMARY

13th West Yorks Regt. VOL XVII Page 1

Original

Place	Date 1917 May	Hour	Summary of Events and Information	Remarks and references to Appendices
ECOIVRES	1.		Marched to MARŒUIL. Cleaned up ready. School for Course of Instruction.	Capt.
MARŒUIL	2		Marched to ST CATHERINES. Took over Maroeuil trenches (Old British front line) Q, b, c. (51B N.W.) Working parties for R.E.'s. Lieut A Hanay. 2/Lt M.P. Phillips to Q.B.C. 11 other ranks wounded by shell.	Capt. Capt. Capt.
IN THE FIELD	3.		In reserve lines Category "B" (reserve of Officer to R) Sent up to Railis. 6 O.R's wounded	Capt.
	4.		Took over trenches at GAVRELLE + WINDMILL C 25 b (51B N.W.) from 16th West Yorks 14th Y.+ L. on left flank 9th Divn on right flank. Very bad weather.	
	5.		Enemy artillery snipers active. Some men of 15th + 16th West Yorks came in from No man's land. Some men wounded. Any Comm: French to Windmill. 2 O.R's killed	Capt.
	6		Capt. L.A.P. Jones O.C. "C" Coy. and 2/Lt. In Arscott wounded (shell storm) Lieut J.A.Henderson took on Command of "C" Coy. 8 other ranks wounded. Shelling at night.	Capt.
	7		Heavy shelling during early morning. 3 O.R's Killed 14 wounded. Rocket prisoner brought in. Relieved by 18th D.L.I. Bivouaced at H.I.C Raining.	Capt.
	8		Moved into Railway Cutting B 27 a. & took over dugouts from 16th W. Yorks. 7 O.R's wounded 1 missing	Capt.

WAR DIARY or INTELLIGENCE SUMMARY

Army Form C. 2118.

Original 13th (S) Bn Yorks & Lancs Regt. XVII Page 2

Place	Date 1917	Hour	Summary of Events and Information	Remarks and references to Appendices
In the Field	May 9.		Took over line behind OPPY. B 18½ T+a. 12½ Y+L. On our right 5th Div on left Naval Bde. Casualties 17 O.Rs wounded.	Appx
	10.		On night of 10.11.17. Bombing parties by "D" Coy 7PM J.S. Sessue in Charge Captures & Consolidates about 120 yards of trench. 8 O.Rs wounded.	Appx
	11.		Capt C.A. Ruston killed by shell. Capt Ainsworth took over duties of Assistant. Enemy artillery active.	Appx
Railway Cutting B 27 a	12.		Support line shewed indimovements. Relieved by 11th East Lancs & took over supports in Railway Cutting B 27 a. "C" Coy attached to 11th East Lancs for support. The Minshewd & 50 O.Rs attached to 176 Coy R.E.	Appx
	13.		Very Quiet.	Appx
	14.		Shell burst near Bn.HQ wounding Lt Col S.E. Milford D.S.O. 4 major D.H. transport Major D.J. Chaout 14 Y+L. took over command. Capt P.M.L. Steel OC "B" Coy took over duties of 2nd in command. Lieut L.O.R. Haygarn took over "B" Coy. Lieut Bowman and 2/Lt North evacuated sick. 10 O.Rs wounded.	Appx
	15.		Collected old bombs etc and attempted to salvage, Pulverised stores to fill ammunition dump over line behind OS 09. Relieving 11th East Lancs who relieved us by 3.0 a.m.	Appx
	16.			Appx

Army Form C. 2118.

WAR DIARY
or
INTELLIGENCE SUMMARY.
(Erase heading not required.)

Original 5th M. Regt Vol XVII page 3

Place	Date 1916	Hour	Summary of Events and Information	Remarks and references to Appendices
	May 16		Egot Leger had a raid which caused the delay Casualties Off 1 killed 2 wounded many Cas of Leutenant Vaughan Sheehan and J. Sybil succumbed to wounds Cal. Leal. 2nd Lts 2nd Lieut took command of A Coy 2nd Lt Shelton to command D Coy Moral "Killing."	Apps Apps Apps
	17		Do	
	18		Do Casualties 2 killed 2 wounded (O.R.)	
	19		10th Dublin Fusiliers came in to report. They reconnoitered the line and received orders from Maj to take over 'C' Coy. This coy losing 2 killed 3 wounded 2 missing. Enemy driven off. Casualties not known. Strength of Coy very heavy.	
	20		Quite quiet during day. Relieved at night by 10th Dublin Fusiliers. Relief was complete at 9 P.M. C=RIVES, had trained and marched to YACOUL	Part Part Apps
	21			Apps
	22		Rested and cleaned up. Lt Creedon went to England on leave. 2nd Lts to 1st Army Repl.	Apps
	23		morning Visit by G.O.C. Division	Apps
	2 P.M.		opening j. N. Brigade Range	Apps
	25		working party for Rifle Range	Apps
	26		Cal. Sun wounded on route to Latrine.	Apps

Army Form C. 2118.

WAR DIARY
or
INTELLIGENCE SUMMARY.

(Erase heading not required.) 8 Yorks Regt. Vol. XVII page 4

Place	Date 1917 May	Hour	Summary of Events and Information	Remarks and references to Appendices
MAROEUIL	27		Marched to FOSSE. sent one coy. & from 15th to Lysts, working lay. & 800 strong	Appx
	28		In GREEN LINE. One casualty. Working lay for GREEN LINE, a new trench. One of coy Borys left tid. Relieved from XII Corps D.T.D.	Appx Appx
	29		Working lay for GREEN LINE. 2 hours farms.	Appx
	30		1 Ord. & 9 O.R. Batt G.P. + 27 O.R. Rel. hospital to duty from 34th I.B.D. Caw Bns while engaged on work making lay. & 300 to GREEN LINE. Brigade Concert in evening tonight. 2.9 O.R. on draft from L Staff casualties for day 2 Officers (killed) wounded	Appx
	31		O.R. 19 130 4 hoses. 18 Gratey reported to VII Corps O.V.P. & relieve 1½ Railway who travelled to ORIVILLE for a course of Signalling	

signature
Lieut Colonel
Commanding 13th York Lancaster Regt.

Confidential

Volume XVIII

Vol 16 99/3

War Diary.

13th Bn. York & Lanc Regt. 31st Division

June 1917

WAR DIARY ~~or INTELLIGENCE SUMMARY~~

Army Form C. 2118.

13th VORX LANCASTER REGT. Vol XVIII

Place	Date	Hour	Summary of Events and Information	Remarks and references to Appendices
ROCKINCOURT	1-1-17		Lieut Col C.B. Wanhope took over Command of the Batt. vice Major F.C. Hoot 2/Lt J.C. Stevenson returned from XIII Corps School of Instruction	924/-
Do	2-1-17		Working party of 300 Green Line. Strength 35 Officers, 793 o.r.	924/-
"	3-1-17		Do Do Do Do Do	924/-
"	4-1-17		Pte Rice 21st Plat. L.C. Course of instruction at Coo Infantry School Lt. Swan & Sheridan to Cr of School for a course in Bombing 2/Lt Boothroyd " " " " Grenades for a course in Signalling	924/-
"	5-1-17		Working party Green Line.	924/-
"	5-1-17		Boxing day	924/-
"	6-1-17		2/Lt G.J. Sutton returned from leave of the United Kingdom. Capt Farr. Wilson returned from leave. Worham Green Line for a party 300	924/-
"	7-1-17		Capt W.G. Wilson with one Coy proceeded to I.D. Camp 2/Lt Parr " " " " " Brigade Sports.	924/-

WAR DIARY
or
INTELLIGENCE SUMMARY.

Army Form C. 2118.

Original

12/3 York Lancaster Reg. Vol XVIII

Place	Date	Hour	Summary of Events and Information	Remarks and references to Appendices
ROCLINCOURT	8-1-17		Work on GREEN LINE working party 800	224
	9-1-17		2/Lt Stevens M.G. O. Joined from Leave	224
	10-1-17		Work on Green Line working party 800. Strength 35 Officers 1053 O.R. 224	
			Batt. once back to Railway Cutting B21C.6 & Pet Bronze Avenue	224
Railway Cutting	10-1-17		Capt. J.T.O. Roberts returned from leave	224
	12-1-17		2/Lt E Parks proceeded on leave to the United Kingdom	224
	13-1-17		Took over the line held by 8 Bay relieving the 11/East Lancs	224
			relief completed by 8 am	
TRENCHES	13-1-17		12/ York Lancaster Regt on our right 5th Div on our left	224
	14-1-17		Our Artillery Bombarded German wire 1 am to 1.30 pm	224
	15-1-17		3 O.R. killed and 6 O.R. wounded	224
			Our Artillery very active 2nd/5 St James & 2nd/7th Sherwood Foresters	224
	16-1-17		Bombarded German line 11.0am to 4 0pm of Infantry.	224
			Strength. 37 Officers 1053 O.R.	
	17-1-17		10 casualties	224
			2 O.R. wounded	
			Our Artillery Bombarded German line 11.0am to 7.0pm	

WAR DIARY or INTELLIGENCE SUMMARY

Army Form C. 2118.

(13th York & Lancaster Reg. Vol XVIII)

Place	Date	Hour	Summary of Events and Information	Remarks and references to Appendices
TRENCHES	17-6-17		In trenches. 2/Lt R Archer and 2/Lt S Laws reported for duty. 2/Lt A. Dawson and Lt F. Ord. ranks reported for duty from 146 Tunnelling Coy.	OBf
	18-6-17		One Artillery wounded German Gun & our 6" & OP. Rifle accidently wounded 2 O.R. wounded	OBf
	19-6-17		Our Artillery active. Relieved by 13th East Yorkshire Regt and proceeded to Nissen Huts Roclincourt. A 28 Central. 1 O.R. wounded	OBf. B24c5.7
ROCLINCOURT	20-6-17		Established and Garrisoned a post of. 2/Lieut B. Holman returns from hospital. Day spent in rest & clean up	OBf
	21-6-17		2/Lt J.S. Liddell returned from hospital. All officers, platoon & section Commanders proceeded to BRUNEHAUT FARM, to meet the C.O. and be shewn over the practice trenches there.	OBf
	22-6-17		Tactical Exercise at BRUNEHAUT FAR. Strength 36 officers 731 OR	OBf

WAR DIARY
or
INTELLIGENCE SUMMARY.

(Erase heading not required.) 13ᵗʰ Yorks Lancaster Regt. Vol. XVIII

Army Form C. 2118.

Original

Place	Date	Hour	Summary of Events and Information	Remarks and references to Appendices
ROCLINCOURT	23-6-17		Tactical Exercise at BRUNEHAUT FARM with the remainder of Bat. Carrying party for same night. Supplies to "B" coy & Lewis gunners.	92A
	24-6-17		Normal Tactical Exercises. Lieut. T. Parker returned from leave to the United Kingdom.	92A
	25-6-17		Inspection of Companies by the Commanding Officer. "B" & "D" Coys. went out tonight covering 2/Lieut. H.P. Stevenson and C.O.R. to inspect the enemy's wire. 2/Lieut. H.S. Stevenson was unfortunately killed by a bullet son after the enemy's normal tour.	92A
	26-6-17		The Bat. relieves part of the 12 East Yorkshire Regt. in the line, half "A" & C coy. in the front line, and the remainder being in support, with "B" coy in reserve. The relief has been necessarily shortened preparatory to an attack. 2/Lieut. L.D.R. Happard while accompanying the C.O. round the line was killed by shrapnel. 2/Lieut. Bagster takes over the duties of Intelligence Officer.	92A

WAR DIARY
INTELLIGENCE SUMMARY

(Erase heading not required.) 13th Yorkshire Regt. Vol. XVIII

Army Form C. 2118.

Place	Date	Hour	Summary of Events and Information	Remarks and references to Appendices
Trenches	26-6-17		Lieut. J. B. Barnes reported for duty from hospital.	
	27-6-17		Enemy front line shelled from 5 p.m. to 7 p.m. The holding of A & B coys. in support moved up to their assembly positions in the front line.	O.K.
	28-6-17		Day spent getting into Battn. into assembly positions. Zero 7.10 p.m. At 7.10 p.m. the three minute barrage from our artillery, after which from 7.13 p.m. the enemy front line & men reached with ease up for casualties as at 7.15 p.m. word reached Battn H.Q. that the objects were found not consolidated in progress. The enemy artillery retaliation barrage was a negligible, & their own the opposing position and parties retained & self enumeration harder to count or number. At 12 midnight "C" coy both over the front line and "A" coy. essential to the reserve line. The Battalions operated on our Right, left was on our Right & our Left was an & Fusiliers, Both these battalions reached their objectives.	O.K.

Army Form C. 2118.

Original

WAR DIARY
or
INTELLIGENCE SUMMARY.
(Erase heading not required.) 13th Yorkshire Regt. Vol XVIII

Place	Date	Hour	Summary of Events and Information	Remarks and references to Appendices
	28(cont)		Our casualties for this day are estimated at 9 killed, 30 wounded, 2 missing.	
	29-6-17		The enemy made no counter attack, but during the day shelled our original frontline with 5.9 and whiz-bangs, the L.T's. and Support trench and the left rear received attention. Our special Coy. over Bat. Battle H.Q. Casualties 3 killed, 18 wounded, includ. 1 officer wounded. The Brigadier visited the trenches, expressed his satisfaction at the work done.	93.
	30-6-17		The enemy artillery was again active on yesterday's targets. During these days carrying parties from the 13th East Yorkshire Regt. were very satisfactory, and to the rear of the attack kept the front companies well supplied with ammunition, R.E. stores etc. During these operations we captured 18 of the enemy & inflicted many casualties on him.	94.

WAR DIARY
or
INTELLIGENCE SUMMARY.

(Erase heading not required.) 13th York & Lancaster Regt. No. 4 v 111

Original

Army Form C. 2118.

Place	Date	Hour	Summary of Events and Information	Remarks and references to Appendices
	30/6		The 11th East Surrey Regt. took over our frontage to 13th Y&L went to the Railway Cutting. Casualties 2 killed and 10 wounded.	984
	3-7-17			

R.W. Curries Major
Commanding
13th S. Batn. York & Lancaster Regt.

Confidential

Volume XIX
No 17

War Diary.

13th York & Lanc Regiment.   31st Division

July 1917

Original

Army Form C. 2118.

WAR DIARY
or
INTELLIGENCE SUMMARY.

(Erase heading not required.) 13th Yorkshire Regt. Vol XIX

Instructions regarding War Diaries and Intelligence Summaries are contained in F. S. Regs., Part II. and the Staff Manual respectively. Title pages will be prepared in manuscript.

Place	Date	Hour	Summary of Events and Information	Remarks and references to Appendices
The Butts	1-7-17		The Batt. was relieved in the evening by the 10th East Yorkshire Regt & proceeded to St Catherines Camp St Catherine	A/Yks
St Catherine	2-7-17		Lieut Colonel Wardrop proceeded to the United Kingdom on leave, Major I Irwin assumed the Batt. from English S.	H A/Yks
BRAY	3-7-17		At 3 pm the Batt. marched off to BRAY. 2/Lt Bond admitted to F.A. The Batt. was paraded then marching in close fatigue order fell out. Divisional Commander who wishes to congratulate them on their took success. During the operation of the 28th, 29th & 30th the casualties were 2 Officers wounded 7 O.R.s killed 69 O.R.s wounded 2 O.R.s missing. TOTAL Casualties 7 killed, 71 wounded 2 missing	A/Yks
BRAY	4-7-17		Training Parades 9.30 am to 12 noon 2.30 pm to 4.0 pm.	H

WAR DIARY
or
INTELLIGENCE SUMMARY

(Erase heading not required.) 13th Yorks Lancs. Regt. Vol. XIX

Army Form C. 2118.

Place	Date	Hour	Summary of Events and Information	Remarks and references to Appendices
BRAY	5-7-17		Usual Training Parades.	
	6-7-17		2/Lieut F.E. Shepperd is struck off the strength of the Batt, having proceeded to Indian Army. 2/Lieuts R.E. Price & C.H. Platt reported for duty from General Inchebald at PERNES	
do	6-7-17		Usual Training Parades	
do	7-7-17		2/Lieut B. Dates reported for duty today. Training as usual. Lieut E.A. Braithwaite returned from General Inchebald's Dispatches.	
do	8-7-17		Celebrating Divine Service 9.30 am.	
do	9-7-17		Training as usual. There was a Roll Count the number of P. and men in the watch, a good muster.	
do	10-7-19		Capt T.G. Bevan returned from Hospital.	
BRAY	11-7-17		Orders arrive to the effect that the Div. is to take over the line from one of the Canadian Divs, and arrive to relieve a C. Batt. meanwhile	

Strength: 33 Officers 618 OR

WAR DIARY or INTELLIGENCE SUMMARY

(Erase heading not required.)

13th York & Lancaster Regt Vol. XIX

Army Form C. 2118.

Place	Date	Hour	Summary of Events and Information	Remarks and references to Appendices
	11-7-17		2 offrs & 7.30 p.m. to NEUVILLE ST VAAST. One officer per company & 1 N.C.O. per platoon leave A.P. to-night for the same. Offrs. to attack fr[ont] on return.	
TRENCHES (ACHEVILLE Sector)	12-7-17		The day spent reading Ops. & the Ret. moved off by platoons at 8.00 p.m. interval one look over 2nd relieving from the Right the 19th York Vancouver Regt on our Right & Post of the 49th Bn. to our Left. The relief was completed about 2 a.m. all quiet. One later relief, although in the LENS & OPPY direction there was the usual artillery activity.	
do	13-7-17			
do	14-7-17		Very quiet day. Lieut. Col. V. B. Waulop returned from leave to UK & he strength on Dukes as usual on 156th front, except for slight shelling of back areas, including Bns. H.Q. Strength: 32 officers 6462 O.R.	
do	15-7-17		2nd Lieut Parker on to Athies, Blecks & offic & Russian trenches on tours of instruction as follows. XIII Corps Infantry school, Lewis Gun course, trenches Mortar course.	
do	16-7-17		Usual activity.	

Army Form C. 2118.

WAR DIARY
or
INTELLIGENCE SUMMARY

(Erase heading not required.) 13th York & Lancs. Regt. C.o.O. XIV

Place	Date	Hour	Summary of Events and Information	Remarks and references to Appendices
Trenches				
"	21-7-17		Slight hostile artillery shelling. Support Trenches. Corporals Quarrel were much relieved to line by the 18th West Yorkshire Regt. Remaining and proceeded to the transport lines for breakfast, thence to WINNIPEG Camp, F 14 8.3 (Ref. map SIGNE 1/40,000)	Yh Ykr
Rest Billet (F 14.8.3)	22-7-17		When about 9 am. The suff of the day was spent in cleaning up, resting. Arr. 3 Mont St. Eloi Road,	
			Capt. T.L. Wood 13th York & Lancs. Regt. took over the duties of Adj. and Capt. A.W. Knowles. Capt. A.W. Knowles proceeded to PARIS been the morning.	
"	23-7-17		Parades: F.d.V. Rifle Inspection adv. lecture of Box Respirators for Chamber	
"	24-7-17		Battle of El Ebon, also training including Drill Musketry and form of specialists. Sports and evening.	
"	25-7-17		Usual trainings Parades. H.E.A. Braithwaite proceeded on Course of Instruction in the use of the Lullaphon at 4th Corps Gas School ORVILLE	
"	26-7-17		General Trenches Parades. Rest Rout march and in morning. The trans. we played the 10th York & Lancaster Regt. at Football, result 3 nil in our favor.	
"	27-7-17		Same Parades except that the chiefs of Town and Funerals at 11am	

WAR DIARY
or
INTELLIGENCE SUMMARY.
(Erase heading not required.)

Army Form C. 2118.

13th Corps Sanne's Post. Cod XIX

Place	Date	Hour	Summary of Events and Information	Remarks and references to Appendices
	16-7-17		Capt W.S. Waller (Instructor) & S. Cpl Anderson R.A.M.C. proceeded to Difflies, their place has been taken by head. Corps' R.A.M.C.	
do	17-7-17		As a result of an C.O. on FRESNOY PARK by Lt Col Bois on 4 supply lines were detailed to relieve unit artillery & Infantry little change taken place & there was no casualties reported from this line. nothing in its situation.	
			No. 8506 R.Q.M.S. Sermith appointed for duty 9.2m of No 5 Sect. The following Soweres & awards have been made to Bad. M.C. Capt. W. Walker D.C.M. Pte J. Lockwood. M.M. Sgt Smearter A.S.T.R. Gydfries H 132, Pte W Bly 1362	
do	18-7-17		No unusual activity. We were relieved in the line by the 11th Batt F laws Regt. thereupon I went back to the Rampart Trenches.	
do	19-7-17		The numerous officers reports for duty 2/Lts Brown, A. Cook, F. Dufton, E.J. Evans — this Cmdt Dunyns into day, the Bad. supplies workmen parties at night.	

Army Form C. 2118.

WAR DIARY
or
INTELLIGENCE SUMMARY.

(Erase heading not required.) 13th Yorkshire Regt. Col XIX

Instructions regarding War Diaries and Intelligence Summaries are contained in F. S. Regs., Part II. and the Staff Manual respectively. Title pages will be prepared in manuscript.

Place	Date	Hour	Summary of Events and Information	Remarks and references to Appendices
Rest Billets	27-7-19 (cont)		The Battalion Sports were held this afternoon. Prizes were presented by Lt. Col. G.B. Wauhope. Capt. W.S. Wilson M.C. returned from tour from course.	
do	28-7-19		Usual training parades.	
	29-7-19		The Batt. marched off from Belair Sot 66 m and took over the Puits marquise trenches from the 18th D.L.I. The relief was complete at 10 p.m. 2nd Lieut. KIRK proceeded to undertake duties on leave this evening.	
Puits (B sub sect) A	30-7-19		The Batt. supplied three companies for working parties on arrangement wiring, the other two companies being kept in the front line.	
	31-7-19		Same working parties as yesterday.	

Strength: 38 Officers 638 O.R.

W. and M —
J.C.
Commdg. 13th Yorkshire Regt.

Confidential

Volume XX

Vol 18

War Diary.

of

13th Bn. York & Lanc. R.

31st Division

August 1917.

Army Form C. 2118.

WAR DIARY
or
INTELLIGENCE SUMMARY.

13th York & Lancaster Regt.

Vol. XX Page 1

(Erase heading not required.)

Instructions regarding War Diaries and Intelligence Summaries are contained in F.S. Regs., Part II. and the Staff Manual respectively. Title pages will be prepared in manuscript.

Place	Date	Hour	Summary of Events and Information	Remarks and references to Appendices
IN TRENCHES near THELUS.	August 1.	—	Finding working parties. Draft of 1 Officer arrived :- 2nd Lieut. J.G. HARRISON.	S/L
	2.	—	Finding working parties.	S/L
	3.	—	Providing working parties. 2nd Lieut. J.S. SIDDELL and 2nd Lieut. M. ASQUITH returned from Hospital.	S/L
BRIGADE RESERVE	4.	—	Relieved the 11th E. LANCS: Regt. in the line, 'ACHEVILLE' SECTOR. Relief Complete :- 12-30 A.M. Lieut. S.B. COUPER R.A.M.C. returned to XIII Corps and was relieved by Capt. M.B. KING. R.A.M.C. Strength: 39 Officers – 640 O.R.	S/L
IN the Line.	5.	—	Battalions on the flanks:- Right = 12th York & Lanc: Regt. – Left = 10th East Yorks: Regt.	S/L
	6. 7. 8. 9.	—	Daily Trench Routine : Situation very quiet on our own front – Considerable amount of wire put out by the Battalion.	S/L
	10.	—	Trench Routine. – Casualties – 1.O.R. KILLED – 4.O.R. WOUNDED.	S/L
	11.	—	Relieved by 11th East Lancs: Regt. in the line. Relief Complete :- 12-midnight. Proceeded to BEEHIVE (Brigade Support) and took over from 12th York & Lanc: Regt. Strength: – 38 Officers – 642. O.R.	S/L
BRIGADE SUPPORT.	12.	—	Finding Working Parties.	S/L
	13.	—	Working Parties.	
	14.	—	Working parties.	
	15.	—	Providing Working Parties. – Capt. F.W.L. HULK returned from Hospital.	S/L
NEUVILLE-ST-VAAST.	16.	—	Relieved at night by 18th Durham Light Infantry in Bde. Support. – Proceeded to Pioneer Camp, NEUVILLE-ST-VAAST.	S/L
	17.	—	Training and providing working parties.	
	18.	—	Training and working parties. – Capt. & Adjt. T.L. WARD left the Battalion and took over the duties of STAFF – CAPTAIN, 94th Inf. Brigade. Strength :- – 3B. Officers. – 641. O.R.	S/L
	19.	—	Working parties.	

Army Form C. 2118.

WAR DIARY
or
INTELLIGENCE SUMMARY.
(Erase heading not required.)

Vol. XX. Page II

Place	Date	Hour	Summary of Events and Information	Remarks and references to Appendices
NEUVILLE-ST. VAAST	August 20.		Working Parties. Draft of 20 O.R. arrived from 34th I.B.D. — There are 53 Reinforcements at XIII Corps. Draft Training Depot — PERNES.	b/s
	21. 22. 23.		Training and working parties. Draft of 1 O.R. arrived.	b/s
	24.		Working Parties.	b/s
In the Line.	24.		Relieved 16th West Yorks. Regt. in the line, ACHEVILLE SECTOR. (L.2. Sub-section.) Battalions on the flanks were:— Right,— 12th York & Lancaster Regt. — Left,— 13th West Yorks. Regt. — Relief complete at 11.45 p.m. Casualties :— 1 O.R. killed — 1 O.R. wounded.	b/s
	25.		Holding the line. 2nd Lieut. H.B. BARNES admitted to Hospital. Strength:— 38 Officers — 712 O.R.	b/s
	26.		Trench Routine. A patrol of 1 officer & 15 O.R. went out to examine enemy wire and surrounded an enemy wiring party. Fire was opened by the enemy wounding one of our men. Our party replied with rifle fire immediately causing casualties.	b/s
	27.		At about 8-15 A.M. three Germans approached our extreme left post (front line), escaping the observations of the day sentry, who was a considerable distance away. One of the enemy entered the trench on the right of the post & shot the nearest man to him & wounding him. Three of our men attacked the Germans & after a struggle succeeded in overpowering him & making him prisoner. The other two Germans escaped. The prisoner belonged to the 6th BAVARIAN. Inf. Regt.	b/s
	28.		At 9-30 p.m. a patrol of 1 officer & 2 sections blew up the enemy's wire with a Bangalore Torpedo & returned about 11-30 p.m. The enemy did not retaliate.	b/s
Brigade Support	29.		Relieved by the 11th East Lancs. Regt. in the line. Relief complete at 11-35 p.m. Took over trenches in Brigade Support — Battalion Headquarters at the BEEHIVE.	b/s
Brigade Reserve	30. 31.		Relieved by the 12th York & Lancs. Regt. in support and took over quarters in Brigade Reserve. Two Companies in EMBANKMENT (VIMY) & two near THELUS. Casualties:— 1 O.R. killed. 1 O.R. wounded.	b/s

Capt. 13th Y & L. Lieut. Col.
Comdg. 13th Y & L. Regt.

Confidential

Volume XXI

Vol 19

War Diary.

13th York Lancaster Regt

31st Division

September 1917.

Army Form C. 2118.

WAR DIARY
or
INTELLIGENCE SUMMARY.
(Erase heading not required.)

1/4th York Lancaster Regt. C Original Vol XXI Page I

Place	Date	Hour	Summary of Events and Information	Remarks and references to Appendices
Thelus Caves	Sept 1st		In Brigade Reserve. Capt A.W. Knowles proceeded on course of instruction to Corps Infantry School of the force to Corps T.M.B. School. Casualties 1 o.r. killed 1 o.r. wounded.	
"	Sept 3rd		"A" C.B. Bomb proceeded to B.H.Q. Lewis gun school, le Touquet. Lt E.A.B. instituted to be A/Captain from 20-7-17.	
L.2 sub sector	Sept 4th Sept 6th		Relieved the 11th East Lancashire Regt in L.2 sub-sector. Relieved by 12th York Lancaster Regt. A Company returned to the 12th Y.L. B Coy in Montreal Trench. C + D Companies in New Brunswick. 2 o.r. killed 2 o.r. wounded.	
A support	Sept 7th		Relieved by the 53rd Canadian Inf Bn. and proceeded to Canada Trench and Red Line in A support and Company relieving a company of the 14th Y.L. and one company a Bn of the Middlesex Regt.	
"	Sept 8-9-10th		Lt. Whitehurst proceeded to First Army Signal School. Apping Ct. Lt Colored Y.B. Wardrop proceeded on leave to Paris Sept 9th 8th. Casualties 3 o.r. wounded. Lt/Cpl Dudley was awarded the Distinguished Conduct Medal	
L.3 sub-sector	Sept 11th Sept 12-17 M.		Relieved 12th York + Lancs in L.3 sub sector. Lt Asquith joined unit & o.r. wounded. Lt Parker proceeded for study at Corps Musketry and Reinforcement Camp. Couples of 2 o.r. on Sept 16/17	
	Sept 18th		t beton on the 14th arrived. Casualties 3 killed 4 wounded. Relieved by the 11th East Lancashire Regt. and proceeded to Mingegate Camp.	
Mingegate Camp	Sept 19-23rd		Carried on training of Companies. Draft of 52 o.r. joined on 19th and 3 o.r. on the 22nd	
B Support	Sept 24-29th		Relieved 12th York + Lancs in B support working parties each day.	
A Support	Sept 30th		Relieved the 12th York Lancasters in A support. B Company attacked to H.Q. Bn M. york + Lancs in the front line. Casualties through gas. 1 26 o.r. wounded	

Confidential

Volume XXI

Vol 20

War Diary.

13th Batt. York Lanc R.   31st Division

October 1917

Army Form C. 2118.

WAR DIARY
or
INTELLIGENCE SUMMARY.
(Erase heading not required.)

13th York and Lancaster Regiment

VOL. XXII.   Page 1

Instructions regarding War Diaries and Intelligence Summaries are contained in F. S. Regs., Part II. and the Staff Manual respectively. Title pages will be prepared in manuscript.

Place	Date 1917	Hour	Summary of Events and Information	Remarks and references to Appendices
RED LINE	Oct. 1 & 2		Providing Working Parties.	
do.	" 3		do.	yes
do.	" 4 & 5		do. Draft of 3 O.R. reported. 2/Lt. Yb. Jones wounded.	yes
FRONT LINE South Sector	" 6		Relieved 12th York & Lancaster Regt. in L3 Sub-Sector. 2 O.R. killed; 4 O.R. wounded.	yes
FRONT LINE South Sector	" 7		Draft of 2 O.R. In Front Line. Draft of 2 O.R. reported. Strength: 31 36 Officers; 1065 O.R.	yes
do.	" 8, 9 & 10		In Front Line.	
do.	" 11		do. The patrol halted when it came to within 100 yards of the enemy's wire. Fire was opened from No. 2 support machine gun. No enemy movements were heard. A patrol of 1 Regt. + 12 O.R. left night of 10/1 + 15 O.R. left our line at 9.0 p.m. proceeded to a point about 50 yards from enemy wire. Sounds of chopping, work and of stakes being driven in were heard. No enemy movements were heard.	yes
	" 12		Relieved by 10th Y. & L. Regt. and proceeded to Springvale Camp. 1 O.R. wounded.	yes
Springvale	" 13		Battalion rested. Lt. H. W. Johnson U.A.M.B. reported for duty.	yes
do.	" 14		Kit inspection. Lt. Col. G. C. Waugh, U.A.R.M.S., 54th Division, proceeded to ETAPLES for Dental treatment. Captain M. G. Yeing M.C., 3rd Officers; 13th O.R.	yes
do.	" 15		Battalion carried on training in the morning; inter-platoon football competition in the afternoon.	yes
do.	" 16		do. do. ; 3 do. do.	yes
do.	" 17		Battalion practised an attack on BRUNHAUT FARM.	yes
" 18			Relieved 12th Y. & L. Regt. in the Brown Line, "B" Support. Provided Working Parties.	yes

WAR DIARY or INTELLIGENCE SUMMARY

Army Form C. 2118.

Vol XXII Page 17

Place	Date 1917	Hour	Summary of Events and Information	Remarks and references to Appendices
BROWN LINE	Oct. 19 & 20		"B" Support. Providing Working Parties. Strength:- 30 Officers; 935 O.R.	
do.	" 21, 22, & 23		do. do.	
RED LINE	" 24		Relieved 13th Y. & L. Regt. in Red Lines. "A" Support. "B" Company in Support to 13th Y. & L. Bn. Lt. Col. G.B. MacIntyre returned from ETAPLES.	
do.	" 25		Working Parties. 2/Lt. WEGODIER and 2/Lt. D.P. MOSBY reported for duty	
do.	" 26		Working Parties.	
do.	" 27		Working Parties. 1 O.R. killed and 5 O.R. wounded near No. 8 Post in NOVA SCOTIA TRENCH. Strength:- 26 Officers; 902 O.R.	
do.	" 28		do. 1 O.R. wounded.	
do.	" 29		do. 2 O.R. wounded. 3 Battalions of the enemy attempted to capture 9th Infantry Brigade's line, with a bombing and bombing attack on our left; 13th East York being attacked on our right.	
FRONT LINE	" 30		Relieved 13th Y. & L. Regt. and moved into Front line for tactical purposes. 8 Officers and 8 sections left our line in front of ACHEVILLE to execute a raid. Two patrols of 80 yards in front of the enemy wire, about 40 yards deep, and two parties were sent out through the enemy wire to patrol his trenches. There was great trouble going through the enemy wire. The bombs were thrown on the patrols right, and great activity was noticed over anemy trenches. The patrol returned at 9:35 pm.	
do.	" 31			

E.O. and J. Smith
Cmdg. 13th Yorks & Lancs Regt.

Confidential

Volume XXIII

X121

War Diary.

13th York Lanc Regt. 31st Division

November 1917.

Army Form C. 2118.

WAR DIARY
or
INTELLIGENCE SUMMARY.
(Erase heading not required.)

13 K. York Lancaster Regt.
Original
Vol. XXIII Page I.

Place	Date	Hour	Summary of Events and Information	Remarks and references to Appendices
In the Trenches.	Nov. 1st	—	Trench Routine. 2 O.R. wounded.	
	2nd	—	Trench Routine. 1 O.R. Killed. 2 O.R. wounded.	
Acheville Sector.	3rd	—	In the Trenches. 2 officers reported for duty. – 2 Lieuts. J.L.GILL & R.E.CLARK.	
	4th	—	Trench Routine. Heavy Artillery cutting wire on front & attached company for a said Heavy Barrage opened on enemy lines at 4-30 p.m. by our artillery supporting raid of Right Division. Considerable retaliation.	
Springvale Camp.	5th	—	Relieved by 14th YORK & LANCASTER Regt. and proceeded to SPRINGVALE CAMP - ECURIE.	R.
	6th	—	Draft of 40 O.R. arrived.	
	7th	—	Rest Day. Cleaning up & Baths.	
	8th	—	Training.	
	9th	—	Training and providing a few working parties.	
	10th	—	DITTO.	
	11th	—	Sunday. Rest Day. Capt. G.H.HUDSON proceeded to U.K. on a months special leave.	
D o.	12th	—	Training. Coy wiring competition won by "C" Coy.	
	13th	—	do. and a few working parties.	
	14th	—	Also working Concertina. Final for Platoon Football Competition won by "Rest of "D". Lt.Col. G.B. WAUHOPE proceeded to U.K. on a months special leave. MAJOR R.W.CURRIN commanding.	
	15th	—	Concertina. 2 Lieut. L.M. MORRIS reported for duty. Lieut. B.P. BURDEE reported	
	16th	—	making for duty, as Medical Officer. (C.U.S.M.C.)	W.
Trenches.	17th	—	Battalion relieved 11th D. LANCS. R. in front line ACHEVILLE SECTOR. "A" Coy Right Front. "C" Coy. Left Front. "B" Support Coy. – 16th D.L.I. on the right. 2 31st CANADIAN Bn. on left.	

Army Form C. 2118.

13th Yorkshire Regt.

WAR DIARY
or
INTELLIGENCE SUMMARY.

(Erase heading not required.)

Original   Vol. XXIII . Page II

Instructions regarding War Diaries and Intelligence Summaries are contained in F. S. Regs., Part II. and the Staff Manual respectively. Title pages will be prepared in manuscript.

Place	Date	Hour	Summary of Events and Information	Remarks and references to Appendices
TRENCHES	Nov. 18	-	Trench Routine. Wiring on the whole front.	
	19	-	Do.	
	20	-	Do. 1. O.R. wounded.	
SPRINGVALE CAMP.	21	-	Relieved by 21st CANADIAN Bn + proceeded to SPRINGVALE CAMP.	
	22	-	Rest Day. Cleaning up and Baths.	
	23	-	Training & Daily Routine.	
	24	-	Do. 2nd LIEUT. S. LEITH reported for duty.	
	25	-	SUNDAY. Rest Day	
	26	-	Battalion Attack Practice. 2 LIEUT W. L. RIVERS reported for duty.	
Trenches.	27	-	Battalion relieved 11th E. Lancs: R. in C.I. OPPY SECTOR. - 'A' Coy. Right Front. 13- E. Yorks R. on Right. - 14th Y. L. on Left. 'B' Coy. Left Front. 'C' Coy. Support. - 115 LEICESTERSHIRE Regt. - Battalion now Commanded by Capt. R. GOODBURN from 14th Y. L. -	
	28	-	Trench Routine. 1. O.R. wounded.	
Do.			Major R.W. CURRIN left to take command of a Chinese attack with dummy figures and smoke bombs took place on BRIGADE front. Enemy retaliated on 'C' Coy with Gas shells but No casualties. Daylight patrol of 1 off. 10 R. was sent out in the morning.	
	29	-	Trench Routine. 1. O.R. Killed. 2 & 5 O.R. wounded.	
#1017.	30	-	Trench Routine. 1. O.R. accidentally wounded. Daylight patrol 1 off. 10.R. sent out.	

R. Goodburn
Capt.
Comdg. 13- York & Lanc: R.

Confidential

Volume XXIV.

M 22

War Diary.

13th Battn York & Lanc Regt.   31st Division

December 1917.

WAR DIARY or INTELLIGENCE SUMMARY

Army Form C. 2118.

13th York & Lancaster Regt

Vol XXIV Aug 1

Place	Date	Hour	Summary of Events and Information	Remarks and references to Appendices
TRENCHES	Aug 1st	-	Usual Routine. 1 Prisoner & 10 OR wounded. Batt Strength 36 officers 718 OR	
OPPY SECTOR	2nd	-	Usual Routine	
	3rd	-	Relieved by 11th E.L. Regt & relieved 12/4/92 in Brigade Support	
	4th	-	Brigade Support	
	5th	-	do	
	6th	-	do	
	7th	-	Relieved in Brigade Support by 4th London Regt & proceeded to Bray	
BRAY	8th	-	Bray Rest day – cleaning up + Baths {2/Lts Popplewell – Ward – Duncan – Aircraft joined for duty. Batt Strength 40 officers 712 OR	
	9th	-	Bray Daily routine & training. 2/Lts Butcher & Yule joined for duty. {2/Lts Everall & Yeo proceeded for duty with Tank Corps Mech. {2/Lt Platt proceeded for duty with M.G.C. Grantham Nos.	
	10th	-	Bray do	
	11th	-	Bray do	
	12th	-	Bray do	
	13th	-	Bray do	
	14th	-	Bray do	
	15th	-	Bray Lt Col Wrangle returned from leave to U.K. & resumed command of Bn from Capt R. Goodbourn. Draft of 30 OR from Base joined for duty. Strength 39 officers 722 OR. 2/Lt Burt joined for duty. 2/Lt Blake proceeded for duty with C.R.E. Boulogne.	

Army Form C. 2118.

WAR DIARY
or
INTELLIGENCE SUMMARY.
(Erase heading not required.)

13th Bork Lancaster Regt
Vol XXIV Page 2

Original

Place	Date	Hour	Summary of Events and Information	Remarks and references to Appendices
BRAY	Dec 16th	—	Training & Daily Routine	
	17th	—	do	
	18th	—	do	
TRENCHES	19th	—	Relieved 21 Canadian Bn in Bdge Support	
ACHEVILLE SECTOR	20th	—	Trench Routine. Working Parties. Lt Skinner & 2/Lt Ashworth joined for duty	
	21st	—	do	
	22nd	—	do Bn Strength 39 Officers 723 O.R. 2/Lt Lurcher proceeded for duty with R.F.C.	
	23rd	—	Trench Routine & Working Parties	
	24th	—	do for wounded	
CUBITT CAMP	25th	—	Relieved in Bde Support by 11th E Lanc Regt & proceeded to Cubitt Camp - Neuville St Vaast. Rest day - cleaning up - Baths.	
	26th	—	Neuville St Vaast	
	27th	—	Xmas dinner	
	28th	—	Training & Daily Routine Captain Holman proceeded to England	
	29th	—	do	
	30th	—	do Bn Strength 38 Officers 720 O.R.	
TRENCHES ACHEVILLE SECTOR	31st	—	Relieved 12th Y & L in Front Line L 2 Sub-sector	

Frankland
Lt Colonel
Comdg 13th York & Lancaster Regt

Confidential

WAR DIARY

13. York & Lancs

Vol. XXVI

Period 1/2/18 to 28/2/18.

Date:- 3/3/18

Army Form C. 2118.

WAR DIARY
or
INTELLIGENCE SUMMARY.

(Erase heading not required.)

Instructions regarding War Diaries and Intelligence Summaries are contained in F.S. Regs., Part II. and the Staff Manual respectively. Title pages will be prepared in manuscript.

Place	Date	Hour	Summary of Events and Information	Remarks and references to Appendices
Front Line	1st		Trench routine. The enemy dropped a barrage on our lines and attempted	
	2nd		a raid on our left flank. Trench Routine	
	3rd		Trench Routine	
	4th, 5th		Trench Routine	
	6th		Relieved by the 11th East Lancashire Regt and proceeded to Hpoegrade Camp	
Hpoegrade Camp	7th		Hpoegrade Camp. Cleaning and inspections.	
	8th, 9th, 10th		Hpoegrade Camp. Training.	
	11th		Hpoegrade Camp. Training. Draft of six other ranks arrived.	
	12th		Relieved the 12th York & Lancaster Regt in Brigade Support. Vancouver Road.	
	13th		In Brigade Support. One other rank killed and one wounded.	
	14th, 15th		In Brigade Support. Trench revetting and working parties.	
	16th, 17th			
	18th		Relieved by 11th East Lancashire Regt and proceeded to Cubitt Camp.	

Army Form C. 2118.

WAR DIARY
or
INTELLIGENCE SUMMARY.
(Erase heading not required.)

Vol XXV page 7

Instructions regarding War Diaries and Intelligence Summaries are contained in F. S. Regs., Part II. and the Staff Manual respectively. Title pages will be prepared in manuscript.

Place	Date	Hour	Summary of Events and Information	Remarks and references to Appendices
Cubitt Camp	19th		Major R. Goodwin returned from leave to the United Kingdom and resumed the duties of 2nd in command.	
	20th		Cubitt Camp training and working parties.	
	21st		Cubitt Camp. 2nd Lieutenant L.F. Davis reports for duty.	
	22nd		Cubitt Camp training and working parties.	
	23rd		Relieves the 12th York & Lancaster Regt in the front line, 1 O.R. wounded and	
	24th		draft of two men from base.	
	25th		Lieut R.H. Wakins posted to R.F.C. on probation. Draft of two men from Base.	
	26th		Draft of 1 O.R. and 1 O.R. killed in action.	
	27th		Trench Routine, 4 O.R. wounded in action 28th	
	28th		Trench Routine. Lt-Col G.B. Wauhope ??? over command of the 9th L Infl Bn	
	29th		vice Brig General T.C. Cartwright-Campbell to England. Major R. Goodison	
			assumes command of the Battalion. 1 O.R. wounded.	
	30th		Relieved by the 11th East Lancashire Regt and proceeded to Springvale Camp.	
	31st		Springvale Camp, cleaning and inspections.	R. Goodwin Major

Army Form C. 2118.

Vol 24

Volume XXVI. PAGE 1

WAR DIARY
or
INTELLIGENCE SUMMARY.
(Erase heading not required.)

Instructions regarding War Diaries and Intelligence Summaries are contained in F.S. Regs., Part II. and the Staff Manual respectively. Title pages will be prepared in manuscript.

Map References: France Sheets 51B and 36B.

Place	Date	Hour	Summary of Events and Information	Remarks and references to Appendices
Springold Camp ECURIE	1918 Feb 1–4		Training.	J.S.
	5		Relieved the 12th York & Lancaster Regt in Brigade dugout, VANCOUVER ROAD. "B" Coy. attached to 14th York & Lancaster Regiment in the line, and accommodated in BRANDON TRENCH. 1 coy of 12th York & Lancaster Regt. attached to this unit and quartered in OTTAWA Rts. One O.R. killed on the 8th inst.	J.S.
	6–10		In VANCOUVER ROAD in Brigade dugout.	J.S.
	11		Relieved by 11th East Yorkshire Regt. and proceeded to LANCASTER CAMP, MONT ST ELOI.	J.S.
	12		LT. A.E. Bramfitt, 2nd Lieuts. H.W. Staff-Brett, E.R. Sudbury, A.G. Monston, L.L. Smith, J.E. Robinson, J.R. Richard and J.J. Tompkins were posted to this battalion from the 14th York & Lancaster Regt. Lt. W.G. Burt, and 2nd Lieuts. E.G. Batten, J.V. Duncan, J. Leith, L.J. Davies, L.M. Morris, R. Walsh and J.G. Yule were posted to the 14th York & Lancaster Regiment. Lieuts. H.B. Wallace; Lieuts. I.B. Westby, B. Klein, E.I. Naylor, and 2nd Lieuts. L. Dickinson, C.B. Kenyon, C.B. Morton, W.J. Purkess, J. Yonge, P. Braggs, H. Gibson, H.W.B. Bamford, D. Barron, H.L. Field, and W. Drury posted to this unit from the 12th York & Lancaster Regt. 50 O.R. were posted to 14th York & Lancaster Regt. 300 O.R. were posted from 12th York & Lancaster Regt. Strength of Battalion – 49 Officers, and 984 O.R.	J.S.
LANCASTER CAMP.	13		Reorganization.	J.S.
"	14–16		Training.	J.S.
	17		Battalion moved to YORK & VILLAGE CAMPS, ECOIVRES. Lieut. Colonel J.B. Wauhope returned from 94th Infantry Brigade and resumed	J.S.

Army Form C. 2118.

Volume XXVI. PAGE II

WAR DIARY
or
INTELLIGENCE SUMMARY.
(Erase heading not required.)

Place	Date	Hour	Summary of Events and Information	Remarks and references to Appendices
	1918 Feby 17		command of the Battalion.	y.S.
	18		2nd Lieut. A.W. Newham reported for duty.	y.S.
	19-23		YORK and VILLAGE CAMPS - training.	y.S.
	24		" " " - Resting, being Sunday.	y.S.
	25-27		" " " - training.	y.S.
	27		Draft of #3 O.R. reported. " 6 Officers and 220 O.R. attached to 146 Tunnelling Coy R.E. - Headquarters at B.10.b.95. (ST NICHOLAS, near ARRAS) " 11 Officers and 166 O.R. attached to 185 Tunnelling Coy R.E. - Headquarters at A.20.b.63. (near ECURIE)	y.S.
	28		The remainder of the Battalion moved back to the FREVILLERS AREA, "A" Company being billeted in FREVILLERS (V.1), the remainder of the Battalion in BAJUS (O.22).	y.S.

Lt. Colonel
Commanding 13th York & Lancaster Regt.

www.ingramcontent.com/pod-product-compliance
Lightning Source LLC
Chambersburg PA
CBHW081438160426
43193CB00013B/2317